# TRAGEDY AND TRIUMPH
## —— on the ——
# TEXAS PLAINS

*Curious Historic Chronicles from Murders to Movies*

## CHUCK LANEHART

*Foreword by Paul H. Carlson*

THE
History
PRESS

Published by The History Press
Charleston, SC
www.historypress.com

*Front cover, clockwise from top left*: author's collection; courtesy Getty Images; courtesy *Lubbock Avalanche-Journal*; public domain; courtesy Southwest Collection, Special Collections Library, Texas Tech University.
*Back cover, top*: Courtesy Southwest Collection, Special Collections Library, Texas Tech University; *bottom*: Ashton Thornhill, Lubbock photographer.

First published 2021

ISBN 9781540247599

Library of Congress Control Number: 2021931017

*This book is dedicated to my muse and trophy wife, Paula;*
*to my favorite daughter, Lindsey; and to Rocky Raccoon.*

# CONTENTS

# CONTENTS

# FOREWORD

Good local and regional history has always been respected—and embraced. Indeed, on many occasions, a former president of Hardin-Simmons University who was also a major Texas historian suggested that all history is local history. Perhaps. And, clearly, that such studies remain fresh and valued can be seen in the success of the extensive list of comparable books from The History Press, including a large number covering towns, places and personalities associated with greater West Texas and its broad prairies and sweeping plains.

Now here comes Chuck Lanehart with his book *Tragedy and Triumph on the Texas Plains: Curious Historic Chronicles from Murders to Movies*. Born in Abilene but reared in the Texas Panhandle, Lanehart, a board-certified attorney and enthusiastic regional historian, has for several years written legal history and biographical studies. His publications include articles in the Texas Criminal Defense Lawyers Association's *Voice for the Defense* and the Harris County Criminal Lawyers Association's *The Defender*. Biographical pieces and other short historic compositions have appeared in the *Lubbock Avalanche-Journal's* "Caprock Chronicles" series. Lanehart also produced a long run of articles on the history of his city's largest country club.

Lanehart's attractive-looking book of thirty-three tightly written essays in seven chapters sits comfortably amid the best recent histories detailing West Texas. In his separate accounts, the author tackles complex legal questions, looks at daring murders and writes of both difficult and festive times. Lubbock, the informal capital of West Texas, is the setting for the bulk of

Lanehart's articles, but he also draws topics from the larger area stretching between the upper Texas Panhandle and the lower end of the High Plains. There is social, cultural and political history presented here, but the major theme, as the title of the book indicates, is biographical in nature.

Lanehart provides fascinating vignettes of colorful characters from both recent and more distant times. He writes about Kit Carson, Quanah Parker, George A. Custer and Temple Houston from the deeper past of the nineteenth century, for example. And from the twentieth century, he looks at such personalities as music and film stars Roy Rogers and Elvis Presley and the highly influential World War II politician George Mahon. Athletes, including famed golfer Ben Hogan and Hall of Fame footballer Bobby Layne, receive attention, as do a whole litany of notorious and dishonorable folks and the agents who brought them to justice.

Altogether an absorbing collection of short, crisp articles, the slim but evocative work offers good reading, interesting stories and unusual tales about the open plains country and its personalities. It may be a regional study, but it is neither provincial nor bucolic. Rather, it is an engaging book that embodies serious history without the scholarly trappings typically associated with critical studies. In the entries presented here, Lanehart is sincere, often profound and always honest. In short, *Tragedy and Triumph on the Texas Plains* represents good, lively history. It is something of a chronicle of West Texas written in essay form. Taken together, the thought-provoking essays make an important and modern contribution to the history of the Texas High Plains.

—Paul H. Carlson
Ransom Canyon

# ACKNOWLEDGEMENTS

I n 1988, my sister-in-law Cindy Martin gave me a faded old photograph from the Southwest Collection (SWC) at Texas Tech University. The photo depicted a curious group of men posing in front of a jail. One sported an eye patch, a few smoked fat cigars, most wore cowboy hats and boots and all seemed dressed in their Sunday best. The caption read, "First murder trial by Jury in Lubbock, 1912." I wondered, "What happened? Who was on trial? What was the verdict?" Thanks to the SWC, my questions were answered, I wrote an article about the case and it was published in a law journal.

Over the years, SWC archivist Monte Monroe—my buddy—and his staff have been invaluable in my research. Many of the stories in this book could not have been written, or illustrated with photos, if not for the immense archive of information stored, organized and readily provided by the SWC.

Paul Carlson, historian extraordinaire, published my first "Caprock Chronicles" article in the *Lubbock Avalanche-Journa* in 2017. He encouraged me to write other articles and inspired me to put this book together.

When Jack Becker took over as editor of Caprock Chronicles a couple of years ago, we immediately bonded, and Jack has published at least one of my articles just about every month. He also indulged my propensity to violate the strict eight-hundred-word limit insisted on by the *AJ*, so I was able to publish several multipart series for the Chronicles.

I practice law for a living. Writing this book meant that my law partner Fred Stangl and my staff—Berna, Tiff, Angie and Mitch—were compelled to cover for me at the office while I wrote and edited my manuscript. Aside from substituting for me at the courthouse when necessary, Fred was especially helpful in the editing process. Berna assisted with formatting, and Mitch was my photo research assistant.

My great friend and photography mentor Ashton Thornhill of Lubbock provided outstanding art for the covers of this book.

Lubbock attorney Charles Blevins, my uber-resourceful friend and colleague, volunteered to troubleshoot technical issues and produce a map for the book.

My brother David Lanehart is a true historian (I am just a writer of "history light") who has written extensively on Native American culture. His gruff criticism of my "soldiers and Indians" stories helped me get them right.

Finally, my muse—trophy wife Paula Lanehart—indulged me by reading every word I have written for this book, gently pointing out my deficiencies while sometimes praising my prose.

# INTRODUCTION

The forty-five-thousand-square-mile Panhandle–South Plains region is immense—about the size of Ohio—and consists of forty-six sparsely populated Texas counties. First inhabited by Clovis man about thirteen thousand years ago, the desolate, arid prairie grudgingly gave way to civilization. It is a place folks still associate with the "Wild West." This book amplifies Wild West preconceptions, debunks misconceptions and throws light on many little-known aspects of the area's history and culture.

Frontiersmen, soldiers and Native Americans clashed on the inhospitable Texas plains of the nineteenth century, spawning countless tales of tragedy and triumph. Those who followed to colonize this lonely land were cattlemen and sodbusters. They also clashed, producing more compelling stories. A rough civilization soon developed on the plains, bringing lawmen and lawyers to deal with inevitable lawlessness, and accounts of legendary legal dramas flourished.

By the turn of the twentieth century, progress on the Texas plains meant establishment of newspapers, followed by moving-picture shows and other forms of cultural evolution. Eventually, the region produced iconic heroes of music, politics and sports.

Famous Wild West names like Carson and Custer will be familiar to readers of this book, though the stories of their Texas plains adventures have largely been overlooked. Forgotten tales of other, less-familiar but equally colorful characters—"Deacon" Jim Miller, "Slippery" Sam Cates, "Poppin" Payne—are recounted here.

The Panhandle–South Plains region of Texas. *Map by Charles Blevins.*

Many of these stories involve classic themes of love and romance, pride and greed, wanderlust and mindless violence. Others are straightforward accounts of history, describing the development of plains culture, including journalism, film, music and politics. These tales begin with Clovis man but primarily involve the period between the establishment of Adobe Walls in the 1840s and late-twentieth century courtroom battles and moviemaking.

Whether heroes or villains, the characters portrayed in the stories that follow were as bold and colorful as the windswept land they fought over, defended and developed. Picture yourself gazing across a nineteenth-century Texas plains battlefield or sitting in a rickety country courtroom balcony, experiencing these exciting tales of the past for the first time.

# 1

# KIT CARSON, QUANAH AND CUSTER

## KIT CARSON, THE COMANCHE AND THE KIOWA ON THE CAPROCK: THE FIRST BATTLE OF ADOBE WALLS

Kit Carson, a frontiersman who ventured throughout the American West, became famous in his lifetime as a gallant army officer, mountain man, guide and explorer. He was well known as an intrepid Indian fighter, but when he appeared on the Texas Caprock to battle Native Americans, he met his match.

By the 1860s, fearsome nomadic Plains Indian tribes had dominated the Llano Estacado for centuries. When wagon trains appeared on the Santa Fe Trail north of the Canadian River in the Texas Panhandle, Comanches with their northern Kiowa allies wreaked havoc on the Anglo travelers, who slaughtered bison and other game the Indians relied on to survive.

In 1863, there was "not a week that whole season, but that some outrage was committed by them," wrote an observer. The Comanches boasted that they would "kill every white man that came on the road." The attacks alarmed U.S. Army general James Henry Carlton, stationed at Fort Bascom in New Mexico Territory. Among those in his command was Colonel Kit Carson, the perfect man to remedy the unrest. The general sent Carson into the heart of Comanche territory on the Texas plains to neutralize the natives and make the area safe for Anglos.

Carlton's orders were simple. No women or children were to be killed, at least not "willfully and wantonly," but otherwise, Carson was free to sanction the Indians as he saw fit. "You know where to find the Indians," Carlton said. "You know what atrocities they have committed. You know how to punish them. They must be made to fear us, or we can have no lasting peace."

Carson's battalion of some four hundred cavalry, infantry and Indian scouts departed on November 10, 1864, with plenty of supplies and two mountain howitzers, hoping to surprise the Indians as they clustered for the winter along the Canadian River. Scouts spotted large encampments of Comanches and Kiowas sprawled on the river's banks. Carson told his officers, "We will have no difficulty finding all the Indians that we desire."

Christopher Houston Carson.
*Public domain.*

On November 25, Carson's cavalry attacked and burned a Kiowa village. Several elderly Kiowas found cowering in their tepees were killed. Other residents fled, scattering to forewarn multiple Comanche encampments nearby.

As Indians planned a counterattack, Carson left 75 infantrymen to protect his supply train and proceeded with about 330 cavalry and scouts to Adobe Walls, an abandoned trading post northeast of present-day Stinnett. The army forces dug in among the ruins and prepared for battle. Soon, a force estimated at between 1,200 and 1,400 Comanche and Kiowa warriors attacked the makeshift fort. One of Carson's lieutenants described the fighters "mounted and covered with paint and feathers... charging backwards and forwards...their bodies thrown over the sides of their horses, at a full run, and shooting occasionally under their horses."

An odd moment of comedy arose during the heat of battle. Months earlier, a Kiowa brave had acquired and learned to play an army bugle. Each time Carson's bugler sounded "advance," the brave—undetected on the dusty battlefield—sounded "retreat," causing great confusion until Carson's men figured out the clever ruse.

Indians kept coming, Carson later wrote, "repeatedly charging my command from different points, but invariably with great loss." They "acted with more daring and bravery than I have ever before witnessed." For hours, waves of warriors attacked Adobe Walls. Carson's men fell farther back to the safety of the ruins, defending their position with furious rifle fire and a determined shelling from the howitzers.

The howitzer barrage repelled the first assault, but a larger force—an estimated three thousand Comanches and Kiowas—soon gathered in what was one of the greatest engagements of Native American warriors ever assembled. Carson was outnumbered ten to one. His troops defended their position for several hours, but Carson had clearly bitten off more than he could chew. He chose his only option: retreat.

Withdrawal was dangerous, as warriors relentlessly attacked Carson's flanks. Comanches started a grass fire, using smoke as a screen to strike without being seen. The soldiers scrambled out of the river valley onto the bluffs, using their howitzers to finally repel the Indians. They stumbled into Fort Bascom before the end of November.

It was Carson's last battle. He later wrote, "The Indians whipped me in this fight." The Comanche-Kiowa alliance had resoundingly driven the great Indian fighter from the field. But it was an encounter that could have ended in a massacre of his men, a disaster that would have dwarfed Custer's last stand twelve years later.

Three soldiers died and another twenty-one were wounded. More than one hundred warriors were killed, with perhaps two hundred wounded. The Kiowa village was decimated.

Kit Carson soon retired, took up ranching and died in 1868 of natural causes at age fifty-eight. The Comanche-Kiowa victory at Adobe Walls gave them control of the Llano Estacado for another decade.

## Plains Indians versus Hide Men: The Second Battle of Adobe Walls

Nothing remains of the ruins, but historic monuments mark a place in Hutchinson County, Texas, known as Adobe Walls, where two celebrated battles—ten years apart—between Native Americans and frontiersmen shaped the future of civilization on the Llano Estacado.

Adobe Walls was a Panhandle outpost established in the early 1840s as a marketplace for Anglo trade with Indians in the area. But by 1848, conflict with aggressive Comanches forced the traders to abandon the fort. They blew the place up with gunpowder. The adobe ruins became a landmark to warn those venturing into dangerous Comanche territory.

Indian uprisings on the Texas plains culminated in 1864 at the First Battle of Adobe Walls. Kit Carson's Union troops stationed in New Mexico Territory rode east, attempting to quell the unrest. When his troops reached the ruins, as many as three thousand Comanches and Kiowas attacked, driving Carson's forces back to New Mexico.

In 1867, some tribes accepted the terms of the Treaty of Medicine Lodge, which required them to relocate to reservations in Indian Territory, which is now Oklahoma. Native Americans understood the ambiguous terms of the treaty as prohibiting "white settlements" in the Panhandle, which they believed was reserved as their exclusive hunting grounds "so long as the buffalo range there in such numbers as to justify the chase." But buffalo hunters—known as "hide men"—continued to exploit the territory. In the 1870s, bison became scarce. The remaining Indians saw this as a serious threat to their existence, and they blamed the illegal hunters. When the federal government failed to intervene, Comanche leader Quanah Parker resolved to drive out the hide men.

In the spring of 1874, Kansas merchants established a buffalo camp near present-day Stinnett in the Indians' hunting territory. Among the twenty-nine occupants were Billy Dixon—the best shot in Dodge City—and twenty-year-old Bat Masterson, a novice hunter. The site was named after the original Adobe Walls one mile away and developed into a center for the buffalo hide trade, with semi-permanent sod structures.

Outraged by this blatant violation of the treaty, Quanah and Kiowa chief Lone Wolf recruited a force of perhaps seven hundred Comanche, Cheyenne and Kiowa braves. Comanche medicine man Isatai'i claimed his magic would make warriors invulnerable to bullets. He promised that a dawn attack would surprise the hunters, who would be annihilated.

Relying on Isatai'i's advice, Indians struck Adobe Walls at dawn on June 27, 1874, but many hunters were awake repairing a broken ridgepole. Dixon described the scene. "There was never a more splendidly barbaric sight. Hundreds of warriors, the flower of the fighting men of the southwestern Plains tribes, mounted upon their finest horses, armed with guns and lances, and carrying heavy shields of thick buffalo hide, were coming like the wind. Half-naked bodies of the riders glittered with ornaments of silver and brass."

The twenty-eight hide men—and a hunter's wife—took cover in two sod stores and a saloon. Initial fighting was at close quarters, with combatants firing handguns as Indians attempted to overrun the village. Thanks to good shooting and the protective earthen walls, the warriors were turned back.

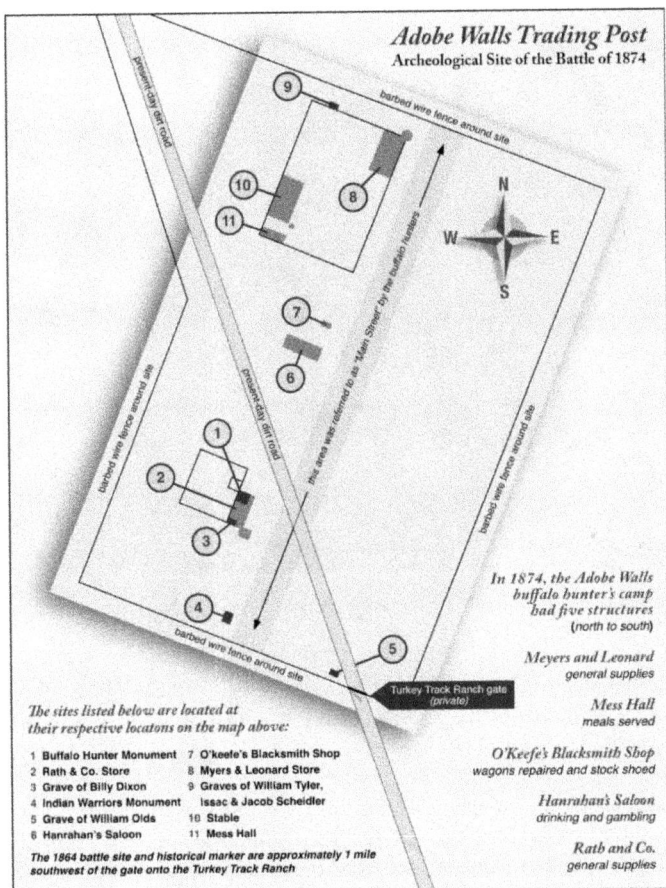

Map of Adobe Walls. *Courtesy Hutchinson County Historical Museum.*

"We tried to storm the place several times, but the hunters shot so well we would have to retreat," Quanah recalled.

The hunters kept the Indians at bay with .50-caliber Sharps rifles, the latest in long-range, high-velocity weaponry. The rifle fire took a heavy toll on the warriors before they could come close enough to return effective

Second Battle of Adobe Walls. *Courtesy Joe Grandee, Historical Western Artist, www. joegrandeegallery.com.*

fire. Quanah's forces encircled the camp for days but made no further attacks. On the third day, a group of braves gathered on a high mesa overlooking the post. Their appearance led to the legendary gunshot of Billy Dixon.

From inside the stockade, Dixon raised his Sharps "Big Fifty" buffalo rifle and knocked a warrior off his horse almost a mile away. Terrified, the Indians soon withdrew, realizing that Isatai'i was a charlatan. The discredited medicine man was beaten and publicly humiliated. Four hide men were lost in the attack, an estimated thirty Indians died and Quanah was wounded. Humiliated by the defeat, Indian bands took revenge on poorly defended targets across the plains. Victims of the attacks demanded military protection, leading to a full-fledged war against Native Americans.

The U.S. Army, determined to eliminate the Indian threat in the region, thoroughly routed the Native Americans in the resulting 1874–75 Red River War.

Quanah and Lone Wolf led their followers to the reservation. Dixon won a Medal of Honor for bravery in the Red River War. Masterson went on to careers as a gambler, lawman and, later, journalist, producing colorful tales of the American West.

As the bison vanished, the dominance of nomadic Plains Indians and their unique lifestyle faded into history. The Texas Panhandle was now safe for ranchers, farmers and other settlers.

## QUANAH PARKER: A MAN OF TWO WORLDS

One of the greatest Native Americans was born on the Texas Caprock, or perhaps in Oklahoma. In either case, Quanah Parker was a legendary presence on the Texas plains and beyond.

Quanah's story begins with his mother, Cynthia Ann Parker, a White child who lived with her pioneer family at the East Texas settlement of Fort Parker in what is now Limestone County. In 1836, Comanches attacked, killing her father and several others and capturing nine-year-old Cynthia Ann, along with two women and two other children.

The other captives were eventually freed, but Cynthia Ann adopted Comanche ways. She married Noconi Comanche warrior Peta Nocona, and Quanah was born of their union in about 1845. A daughter, Prairie Flower, came later. Quanah believed that Oklahoma was his birthplace, but there is evidence that he was born near Cedar Lake, northeast of Seminole, in Gaines County.

In 1860, at the Battle of Pease River, in what is now Foard County, Texas Rangers and federal troops encountered the Noconi and found Cynthia Ann and Prairie Flower among them. Seven Indians were killed, and Cynthia Ann and Prairie Flower were taken by the federal troops. Teenage Quanah, who was not present at the battle, was taken in by the Quahada Comanches of the Llano Estacado and never saw his mother again.

Cynthia Ann was welcomed by the Parker family but never fully adjusted to White ways. After Prairie Flower died in 1864, Cynthia Ann became increasingly embittered over her lost children, eventually starving herself to death in 1870.

Meanwhile, Quanah became known among the warlike Quahadas as an accomplished horseman and a budding leader—ruthless, clever and fearless in battle. He rejected treaties with the United States that relocated Native Americans to reservations in Indian Territory, now Oklahoma.

As other tribes agreed to government terms, Quanah's people continued their traditional nomadic existence, chasing bison across the Texas plains.

Those who trespassed on the Llano Estacado were raided and punished. In a campaign to find and subdue the elusive Indians, U.S. Army colonel Ranald Mackenzie's troops reached Blanco Canyon in Crosby County in 1871. It was the first such expedition to venture so deep into Comanche territory.

Quanah's warriors attacked at midnight, stampeded some seventy of the cavalry's best horses and mules through the encampment, then disappeared. Mackenzie—namesake of Lubbock's Mackenzie Park—soon gave up his search for the Quahadas. One of Mackenzie's officers described Quanah in battle: "A large and powerfully built chief led the bunch, on a coal black racing pony. Leaning forward upon his mane, his heels nervously working in the animal's side, with six-shooter poised in the air, he seemed the incarnation of savage, brutal joy."

In the spring of 1874, merchants established a buffalo hide trading post at Adobe Walls in the Texas Panhandle. Quanah believed the settlement was a violation of the Medicine Lodge Treaty, which reserved the area as exclusive Indian hunting territory.

On June 27, 1874, Quanah led an attack on the post by combined forces of about seven hundred Comanche, Kiowa and Cheyenne warriors. They were turned back by twenty-eight well-armed buffalo hunters, but other less-fortified sites across the plains soon felt the Indians' wrath.

The Red River War followed, and Mackenzie returned. In the September 1874 Battle of Palo Duro Canyon, his forces destroyed Native American villages, killed some fifteen hundred Indian horses and wiped out their winter provisions. Only four braves died, but this last battle of the Texas Indian wars brought Comanche domination of the plains to an end.

In 1875, Quanah's people were the last Texas tribe to surrender. He led the hungry Quahada people to a reservation in southwestern Indian Territory. Soon, he was named chief, and Quanah oversaw the transition with remarkable ease, busying himself uniting the various Comanche bands. He worked to promote self-reliance, supported construction of schools and encouraged young people to learn the White man's ways.

Quanah endorsed agriculture and became a cattleman. He served as judge on the tribal court, negotiated agreements with White investors and fought attempts to revert to traditional ways.

But Quanah did not abandon all tradition, refusing to cut his long braids and maintaining a twenty-two-room home for his seven wives and numerous children. He followed the teachings of the peyote-eating Native American

Quanah Parker. *Public domain.*

Church and encouraged peyote use among his followers. "White man goes into his churches to talk about Jesus," Quanah said. "The Indian [goes] into his tepee to talk to Jesus."

Quanah was perhaps the wealthiest Native American during his lifetime and bonded with the rich and powerful, including President Theodore Roosevelt and iconic Panhandle rancher Charles Goodnight.

In 1901, the federal government divided the Kiowa-Comanche reservation into individual holdings and opened the area to settlement by outsiders. Still, Quanah maintained his position as the most influential of the now-dispersed Comanches, operating his profitable ranch and continuing to seek business ties with Whites.

Quanah died in 1911 and was buried in full Comanche regalia beside his mother and Prairie Flower at Post Oak Mission Cemetery near Cache, Oklahoma. Their graves were later relocated to Fort Sill.

# Custer, Captive Girls and the Cheyenne
## on Sweetwater Creek

George Armstrong Custer stands alone as the most famous—and infamous—of American Indian fighters. He is remembered for his heroism—and lack of leadership—in the disastrous 1876 Battle of the Little Bighorn. But before "Custer's Last Stand," he visited the plains of Texas, with much different results.

Decorated twenty-five-year-old Union general Custer arrived in Austin in 1865 as part of occupation forces following the Civil War, commanding the Second Division of Cavalry, Military Division of the Gulf. During his Texas assignment, Custer's volunteer troops threatened mutiny, preferring to be mustered out of the army rather than continue the postwar Texas campaign. They resented Custer's imposition of harsh discipline and considered him nothing more than a "vain dandy."

In early 1866, Custer left the army and returned to civilian life, but he soon rejoined the military at a lower rank. Custer was appointed lieutenant colonel of the newly created Seventh Cavalry Regiment in July 1866. Headquartered at Fort Riley, Kansas, the unit was tasked with forcing Plains Indian submission to federal authority.

Two years later, a lonely Custer abandoned his post to visit his wife of four years, Libbie. He was arrested, court-marshalled and sentenced to serve a year in custody at Fort Leavenworth. General Philip Sheridan needed Custer for his winter campaign against noncompliant Cheyenne and arranged for Custer's early reinstatement in October 1868. The two led expeditions in Kansas and Indian Territory (Oklahoma) against the Southern Cheyenne, a serious threat to White settlers.

Meanwhile, pretty, auburn-haired teenager Sarah Catherine White of Kansas was taken from her family in August 1868 by Cheyenne renegades. Her father was killed in the attack. Two months later, Anna Brewster Morgan's Kansas homestead was attacked by Sioux warriors. They shot her husband, James, and spirited the twenty-four-year-old away, soon trading her to the same group of Cheyenne holding Sarah White. The two girls bonded, but both were subjected to "unspeakable abuse" by their captors.

In November, Custer led his troops in an attack on a Cheyenne encampment on the banks of the Washita River, just east of the Texas Panhandle border in Oklahoma. Custer's forces killed 103 warriors and some women and children; 53 women and children were taken as prisoners. One of the Cheyenne girls captured, Meotzi, was described

*Right*: Lieutenant Colonel George Custer, commander of the Seventh Cavalry Regiment, circa 1869. *Public domain*.

*Below: Battle of the Washita River* by Steven Lang. *Courtesy National Park Service*.

by Custer as "enchantingly comely." She became his lover, visiting his tent every night, according to Cheyenne folklore and accounts by officers in Custer's command.

Custer had his men shoot most of the 875 Indian ponies they captured. The Battle of Washita River was the first substantial U.S. victory in the Southern Plains War, forcing many Native Americans onto reservations. Historians describe the battle as a brutal massacre.

In early 1869, Custer scoured the Llano Estacado for Cheyenne. A three-week excursion along the Prairie Dog Town Fork of the Red River in the eastern Texas Panhandle was unsuccessful. Next, he headed farther north.

West of Indian Territory in what is now Wheeler County, Texas, the Sweetwater Creek flowed. The waterway was essential to millions of southern American bison in a region known as Comancheria. The area was beautiful, with lush grass, sprouts and rugged shrubs providing fodder for ponies. Thick outgrowths of big cottonwood trees offered fuel in winter and shade in summer. Elevations on either side of the creek protected those below from the unforgiving climate of the Panhandle. Plains Indians camped along the freshwater stream to seek shelter from harsh winters as Anglos continued to settle the southern plains.

On March 15, 1869, Custer's scouts located a Cheyenne village of 260 lodges near Sweetwater Creek. Custer proceeded peacefully to the village, hoping to forge a truce. He was escorted into the tepee of Rock Forehead, the Cheyenne mystic and chief, and learned that Sarah and Anna were in his custody. It was joyous news for Daniel Brewster, Anna's brother. Earlier in the campaign, he had volunteered as a scout for Custer, hoping to find his sister or learn of her fate.

Custer sat among the chiefs, smoked a large ceremonial clay pipe and talked of peace. The Cheyenne were eager for peace, as harsh winter treks had weakened their people and their ponies. Before Custer stood, Rock Forehead sprinkled tobacco ash on the commander's boots and chanted, prophetically, "If you act treacherously toward us, some time you and your whole army will be killed."

Custer replied, "I will never kill another Cheyenne." Satisfied, Rock Forehead directed him to a suitable spot to encamp.

With Meotzi acting as interpreter, the foes negotiated for three days about the release of the White captives and the Cheyenne's surrender to the reservation. When the Indians tried to flee, Custer took three chiefs prisoner and threatened to hang them unless the White girls were freed.

Custer dramatically hung ropes across a cottonwood limb and placed the chiefs nearby as the Cheyenne watched. Chief Rock Forehead relented, promising to free Sarah and Anna and report to the reservation as soon as their ponies could make the journey. Custer pledged to free the three chiefs and the women and children captured at Washita. The Kansas girls were released, passing through a double line of jubilant soldiers. Anna's brother Daniel lunged forward, breaking into a run. Dashing through the line, he pulled his sister into a massive hug. "Oh, sister, how you must suffer!"

An officer recalled, "The larger one appeared to be 50 years old, though she was less than 25. She was stooped, pale and haggard, looking as if she had been compelled to do more than she was able. She was quite tall, with light hair that was bleached on top until it was dirty brown from exposure. Her clothes were made of three or four kinds of material, pieces of tents and blankets, all worn out and sewed together with strings."

Soldiers threw off their great coats to comfort the girls. Custer wrote, "Men whom I have seen face death without quailing found their eyes filled with tears, unable to restrain the deep emotion produced by this joyful event."

Overwhelmed by their freedom, the girls pulled each other into a hug. Custer reported, "Both wore their hair in two long braids, and as if to propitiate us, the Indians, before releasing them, had added to the wardrobe of the two girls' various rude ornaments, such as are worn by squaws. About their wrists they wore coils of brass wire; on their fingers had been numerous rings, and about their necks strings of variously colored beads."

The women were escorted to an officer's tent. Custer's cook took them under her charge and dressed them in more suitable clothing, pieced together from her wardrobe and a selection of calico. Anna described their horrific ordeal. "The Indians subjected us to the most cruel treatment, frequently beating us in the most savage manner."

Custer refused to release his hostages until the Cheyenne made good on their promise to surrender to the reservation. But Rock Forehead's people continued their traditional nomadic lifestyle, pursuing buffalo across the plains. Eventually, Rock Forehead's tribe surrendered to the reservation, but he fled and died peacefully in Montana in 1875, age eighty-one.

Two of the Cheyenne chiefs captured at Sweetwater Creek were killed in a confrontation with soldiers, but the third chief and the Washita women and children were released to the reservation. Among the Cheyenne captives released was Meotzi, Custer's lover following her capture.

Anna Morgan returned to her home in Solomon Valley, Kansas. She was warmly welcomed by her husband, James, who had recovered from his wounds in the Sioux attack when Anna was abducted. In late 1869, Anna delivered a half-Cheyenne son she named Ira. Unfortunately, Ira died before age two. After Anna and James had three children, they divorced. She never recovered from the trauma of her capture and died at age fifty-seven in 1902 in a Topeka mental institution.

Sarah White moved to Cloud County, Kansas, and became a schoolteacher. She married Erastus Otis Brooks, and they had seven children. In 1874, she petitioned the U.S. government for compensation for her ordeal. It was denied. Sarah died in 1939 at age eighty-eight.

Seven years following his dramatic rescue of Sarah and Anna, Custer and his Seventh Cavalry found themselves surrounded by a superior force of Lakota Sioux, Northern Cheyenne and Arapahoe near the Little Bighorn River in Montana Territory. In the resulting battle, some 275 soldiers were killed, including Custer, in the greatest U.S. military defeat of the Indian Wars. He was thirty-six years old.

There are claims that Meotzi was present at the Battle of the Little Bighorn with her son, born of her union with Custer. Some historians argue that Custer was sterile and the child's father was instead Custer's brother Thomas Custer, who also died at Little Bighorn. Meotzi is said to have protected Custer's body from mutilation. Another account claims that Meotzi was not at the battle, but two Southern Cheyenne women who were present recognized Custer's body as being Meotzi's husband and protected it. Following Custer's death, Meotzi cut her hair and slashed her arms and legs.

According to a 2008 book by Gail Kelly-Custer, who claims to be a direct descendant of Custer and the Cheyenne maiden, Meotzi married a White man named John Isaac, changed her name to Mary and died in Oklahoma in 1921.

A year following the battle, Custer's remains were found at the battlefield in a shallow grave near the bodies of forty of his men, including his brother and nephew, and dozens of dead horses. He was buried with full military honors at West Point. His widow, Libbie, who had accompanied Custer in many of his expeditions, wrote several books that advanced his stature as a heroic military leader.

# 2

# KILLINGS AND CONTROVERSIES OF THE TEXAS PLAINS FRONTIER

## SOLVING THE FIRST HOMICIDE ON THE SOUTH PLAINS

In 1900, thousands of cattle grazed vast ranches on the South Plains of Texas, but humans were few and far between. Lubbock County residents totaled less than three hundred. A few dozen ranchers occupied the unorganized counties west of Lubbock.

But changes were coming. In 1895, the Texas legislature passed the Four Sections Act, authorizing homesteaders to purchase four sections of land (2,560 acres) from the state under very favorable terms. Small entrepreneurs scurried to take advantage of the wonderful opportunity. Among them was James William Jarrott.

Jarrott was born in Alabama in 1862, but his family soon moved to Texas. In 1886, he married Mollie Wylie, a beauty from Hood County, and the couple moved to Weatherford.

Representing his area, Jarrott served in the Texas House of Representatives and there won respect among his peers, developing a reputation as "fearless in speech." He met fellow legislator Charles Rogan, soon to play a pivotal role in the settlement of the Llano Estacado.

After Jarrott left the legislature, the family moved to Stephenville, where he studied law and was admitted to the bar. Although elected Erath County attorney, he was restless. Early in 1900, he traveled to Plainview to visit relatives, exploring the windswept, treeless Llano

James and Mollie Jarrott.
*Courtesy Southwest Collection,*
*Special Collections Library,*
*Texas Tech University.*

Estacado. Afterward, he heard important news from his friend Rogan, now the Texas land commissioner.

Rogan had discovered a slice of state-owned land west of Lubbock that had not been surveyed. He intended to place the land for sale under the terms of the Four Sections Act. However, the act required the land to be surveyed. Jarrott paid for the survey, gaining an advantage over others coveting the land, soon to become known as "The Strip."

The Strip extended westward sixty miles from the western boundary of Lubbock County. It crossed the unorganized counties of Hockley, Terry, Cochran and Yoakum, reaching in a narrow band to the New Mexico border.

Jarrott recruited twenty-four families from the Erath County area to join him, Mollie and their children on the arduous three-hundred-mile horse-and-wagon journey to the almost vacant South Plains. Each family claimed four sections of fertile land. It was May 1902.

Cattlemen previously established in the area did not greet the settlers warmly. Ranchers had long grazed cattle on the grassy unfenced Strip. They threatened violence, withheld precious water from windmills and filed lawsuits against the "nesters," claiming that Jarrott had unfairly failed to share his survey with ranchers. Among Jarrott's chief rivals were ranchers from the Lake-Tomb Cattle Company.

In far-flung courthouses across the plains, Jarrott defended the settlers against the ranchers. He won all the lawsuits. He traveled to Austin to assert the settlers' rights in the Texas Land Office. By August, the settlers were legally established on the Strip.

On August 27, Jarrott left Mollie and their children at Lubbock's Nicolett Hotel, where Mollie was recovering from an illness. The unarmed lawyer was bound for their homestead on the Strip in Hockley County. He never returned. Someone found Jarrott's lifeless body lying in a stock tank near present-day Ropesville on land owned by the Lake-Tomb Cattle Company. He had been shot to death. Jim Jarrott was forty-one years old. It was the first documented homicide on the Texas South Plains and went unsolved for more than a century.

Those responsible for Jarrott's death thought the nesters would be scared away, but they were wrong. The settlers persisted.

Burdened with three young children, Jarrott's thirty-six-year-old widow, Mollie, developed the land that had cost her husband his life. She expanded the original claim to sixteen sections and raised a prime herd of cattle. Mollie married a second time, to real estate developer Monroe Abernathy. Mollie and Monroe were instrumental in bringing the railroad to Lubbock in 1909, and Mollie is considered Lubbock's first businesswoman.

Descendants of the Jarrotts, the Abernathys and other Strip settlers still reside on the South Plains.

But who killed James Jarrott? The assassin was "Deacon" Jim Miller, one of the most infamous gunmen of the era, responsible for perhaps fifty-one killings. Shortly before his death in 1909, Miller confessed to killing Jarrott, saying he was paid $500 for the murder. But he never named his employer.

The man who hired Miller to kill Jarrott was probably M.V. "Pap" Brownfield, a powerful rancher allied with the Lake-Tomb Cattle Company. Until recently, Pap, who died in 1929, was not suspected of the crime. But a careful review of one-hundred-year-old deed records and other court records in 2014 clearly linked Miller to Brownfield and Jarrott's assassination. Ironically, the assassin's fee was likely covered by the deed to a plot of land that eventually became the city of Brownfield, named in Pap's honor.

By contrast, the man who brought the first wave of settlers to the South Plains is largely forgotten. There is no town, no school, no street named in honor of James William Jarrott. That is a shame.

## THE BADDEST OUTLAW OF THE WEST

Many infamous outlaws terrorized the Old West, gunslingers like Billy the Kid and John Wesley Hardin. But one name stands out as the most efficient, elusive killer of the bunch: Jim Miller. His dastardly deeds included the first documented murder on the South Plains.

Miller's homicidal exploits—from central Texas to New Mexico to West Texas to Indian Territory—resulted in the deaths of as many as fifty-one men, by Miller's own count.

Soon after his 1861 birth in Arkansas, Miller's family moved to central Texas. At age eight, Miller was suspected of murdering his grandparents, but the boy was too young to be prosecuted. In 1884, he was indicted for the shotgun slaying of his brother-in-law, John Coop. A Coryell County jury sentenced Miller to life in prison, but the conviction was overturned on appeal.

He drifted through southeast New Mexico, bragging, "I lost my notch stick on sheepherders I killed on the border."

By 1891, Miller was living in Pecos. Bad blood developed between Miller and the local sheriff, Bud Frazer. In 1896, Miller cornered Frazer in a saloon. As bystanders watched, he killed Frazer with two shotgun blasts. The case was transferred to Eastland County. To prepare for trial, Miller moved to Eastland, where he lived peacefully with his family, attending church regularly.

The community came to accept the Millers, and Jim's churchgoing ways won him a paradoxical nickname: "Deacon" Jim Miller. An Eastland jury

"Deacon" Jim Miller. *Courtesy Fred R. Maxey Jr.*

acquitted Miller of the Frazer murder on a plea of self-defense.

Miller stood an inch over six feet tall, with black hair, gray eyes and a dark complexion. He assumed the appearance of a pious Methodist, with ramrod-straight posture and impeccable attire. He did not curse, nor did he smoke or drink.

At some point, Miller changed roles from a common murderer to a contract killer.

In 1900, lawyer James Jarrott began recruiting central Texas families to settle grassland west of Lubbock pursuant to the Four Sections Act. The arrival of Jarrott's two dozen small agricultural families angered cattlemen who grazed livestock on the open range. Powerful ranchers brought lawsuits against the "nesters." Among Jarrott's adversaries was Pap Brownfield, patriarch of an influential South Plains ranching family.

Jarrott prevailed in the litigation, legally establishing his clients on land in Hockley, Terry and Cochran Counties.

Meanwhile, Miller arrived on the South Plains, engaging in a shady real estate deal with the Brownfield family in Terry County, flipping land for a windfall profit, compensation for an assassination.

On August 27, 1902, Jarrott was ambushed as he rode from Lubbock to his claim in Hockley County. His lifeless, bullet-ridden body was found in a pond near present-day Ropesville. Jarrott, forty-one, was the first recorded South Plains murder victim.

Miller later confessed to Jarrott's assassination, confirming that he was paid $500 to eliminate the tenacious lawyer, "the hardest man I ever had to kill." But he never named Brownfield or anyone else as his employer and died before charges could be brought.

For one hundred years, the shady money-laundering transaction successfully obscured proof that Miller's fee for murdering Jarrott came from Pap Brownfield. But a close examination of old court filings and deed records in 2014 clearly revealed the connection between Miller and Brownfield and their likely conspiracy to kill Jarrott.

In Indian Territory, Clint Pruitt hired Miller to avenge the shooting of his brother by Deputy U.S. Marshal Ben Collins. In 1906, the marshal was assassinated by a shotgun blast. Miller was arrested and indicted for Collins's murder but was released on bail and was never tried for the murder. He was suspected of assassinating former lawman Pat Garrett—slayer of Billy the Kid—in Las Cruces, New Mexico, in 1908, though historians question Miller's connection to the crime.

Early in 1909, Miller arrived in the bustling boomtown of Ada, Oklahoma. A bitter feud had developed between saloon operators and former Deputy U.S. Marshal Gus Bobbitt. The saloon owners employed Miller to settle the matter. Soon, Bobbitt was dead from shotgun fire. Miller and his co-conspirators were jailed, but Miller's reputation for beating murder raps alarmed Ada's citizenry. A mob dragged the prisoners into an abandoned livery stable.

Before he was hanged, Miller said, "I've killed fifty-one men." He asked that his diamond ring be left for his wife and his diamond shirt stud be given to a friendly jailer. He requested his coat and hollered, "Let 'er rip!"

A photographer captured the aftermath of the grisly scene, and postcards of the lynching were proudly hawked by Ada merchants for decades. The baddest outlaw of the West was dead.

# The Last Hanging in the Panhandle

Fiction and film are filled with fables of condemned killers and horse thieves publicly hanged on town squares across the vast plains of Texas. But only one man was legally hanged on the Texas plains. The compelling legend of G.R. Miller is called "the last hanging in the Panhandle," which is true, but it was also the first. No report exists of any other legal hanging in the recorded history of the Panhandle–South Plains.

It seems ironic that the execution took place in the peace-loving Donley County town of Clarendon. Early settlements of the Panhandle included only three towns: Tascosa, Mobeetie—now ghost towns—and Clarendon. Tascosa and Mobeetie easily matched violent Hollywood notions of the Wild West, yet there were no hangings in those towns. Clarendon was different. The town founder was a Methodist minister who envisioned a "sobriety settlement" in contrast to typical boomtowns of the era. No saloons or brothels existed in the little town that disappointed cowboys called "Saint's Roost." Yet, in 1910, gallows appeared near Clarendon houses of worship for the first—and only—time in the history of the Panhandle–South Plains.

In 1909, G.R. Miller was a thirty-two-year-old farmer and miner from Acme in Hardeman County. His parents had emigrated from England. Miller was slim, about five feet, nine inches tall and a chain-smoker. With light complexion, blue eyes and dark hair, he was described as handsome. He could read and write but attended only four years of school.

Miller was a small-time criminal who stood trial for a Hardeman County forgery two years earlier. Physicians and jurors were convinced he was "of unsound mind," but he was nonetheless convicted and sentenced to two years in prison. There, he was considered "excessively out of control" and punished with twenty lashes.

The crazy inconsequential criminal would soon generate front-page headlines for much more heinous crimes.

Shortly after his release from prison, while working at a gypsum mine near Childress, Miller devised a sinister scheme. He stole dynamite from the mine and blew up a friend's home as a decoy for robbing his paymaster's office. The plan failed. He stole a pistol from a relative and fled, hopping a westbound freight train. It was March 20, 1909.

Two hobos boarded the boxcar Miller occupied. He pulled his stolen .38 revolver and fired twice. One man's skull exploded. He shot again and nicked the earlobe of the second hobo, who escaped through the open freight door.

Miller pulled a half-dollar from his victim's pocket and pushed the dead man into the Red River at Estelline in Hall County. The body was found the next day, but neither hobo was ever identified.

Miller fled the bloody boxcar and jumped on another freight car of the same slow-moving train, where he was greeted by two friendly vagabonds from Fort Worth. Cousins Floyd Autree and Fred Garrett, both in their early twenties, were headed to Amarillo for work. They had not heard the shooting for the roar of the train. The trio seemed to get along, sharing cigarettes as Autree played harmonica in the semi-darkness of the early morning. As the train neared Clarendon, Miller suddenly pulled his pistol and shot Autree in the head. He fired at Garrett but missed, and the boy jumped from the boxcar.

Garrett ran toward the caboose and got the attention of railroad authorities. By the time the train stopped and they reached the boxcar, Miller had fled and Autree was clinging to life. He died later that evening in a Clarendon hotel.

Miller had searched Autree's pockets, found nothing and walked to Rowe, in southeastern Donley County. That afternoon, lawmen arrested him in Rowe without incident. Miller was carrying the pistol, dynamite and correspondence to a Boston establishment: an order for a wig and false whiskers, to be mailed to him in Dalhart.

Soon, Miller confessed to the murders. Miller's gory rampage was front-page news throughout Texas and beyond. The sheriff feared a lynching and jailed Miller safely in Claude, thirty miles west. On May 31, in Memphis, Miller's trial for the murder of the anonymous hobo began. Miller's mother and other relatives testified, pleading for mercy, but he was convicted and sentenced to life in prison. He was transported to the state penitentiary to await his next murder trial.

Miller's trial for the killing of Autree began on November 1 in Clarendon. Before a packed courtroom, the indictment was read, and without emotion or hesitation, Miller pled guilty. His lawyers presented an insanity defense, which was rejected. After fifteen hours of deliberation, the jury found Miller guilty and sentenced him to death.

Appeals were unsuccessful, and his execution was scheduled. Miller was to be hanged on the morning of June 3, 1910, in the peaceful town of Clarendon.

Awaiting execution, G.R. Miller became a popular contributor to the local newspaper from his Clarendon jail cell. The doomed man authored an invitation asking townspeople to meet him at the gallows so he could

The Donley County Courthouse, site of G.R. Miller's death sentence for killing Floyd Autree of Fort Worth, 1910. *Courtesy Clarendon Enterprise.*

tell them he forgave them. He began to write poetry and sent a long ballad to the editor about his life of crime. Another poem, written about prison life, was especially poignant, "What is life without liberty / I oft times have said / With a poor troubled mind / It is always in dread." Clergymen often visited Miller in his cell. Three days before his execution, he was baptized into the Catholic faith.

A scaffold was constructed at the edge of town. Days before Miller was to be hanged, visitors began arriving in Clarendon by train, buggies and wagons, on horseback and on foot. Extra lawmen were called in, nervously monitoring the crowd. Campfires illuminated the area well into the night.

On the morning of June 3, 1910, Clarendon took on a festive atmosphere. Food vendors hawked their wares, and many visitors brought picnic baskets. Though women were banned from attending the execution, one thousand area men and boys gathered near the gallows.

Law officers escorted Miller through the crowd to the scaffold in a covered buggy, accompanied by physicians, a Catholic priest and a Methodist minister. He was smartly dressed in a dark suit and white shirt. Miller faced the huge crowd, thanked those who had helped him and forgave those who were punishing him. He said, "I humbly and sincerely ask forgiveness for the scandal and bad example I have given by my past wicked life and I hope that none will follow my example."

The condemned killer seemed calm, but his voice began to falter as he uttered his final words. "All you children be good children," he said. Then he mumbled something about not crying over spilt milk. Miller turned to the sheriff, heartily shook his hand, thanked him and said he was ready.

At 11:00 a.m. a black cap sewn by the sheriff's wife was slipped over the killer's head, the noose was adjusted, the trapdoor was sprung and he plunged six feet into the shed below with a broken neck. Thirteen minutes later, physicians declared Miller dead. His body was placed in a horse-drawn hearse, and spectators watched as he was carted away with his feet protruding from the end of the funeral coach, too short for the corpse.

The crowd purloined pieces of the noose and scaffold as souvenirs before it was dismantled.

Catholic services were held for Miller the next day, and he was buried in an unmarked grave in a small Catholic cemetery south of Clarendon.

On June 4, the local newspaper editor took great pains to report the hanging "without pandering to the curiosity of those whose minds could

The hanging of G.R. Miller, the last hanging in the Panhandle–South Plains region, 1910. *Courtesy Clarendon Enterprise.*

be unduly influenced by recital of sensational and spectacular happenings." The editor wrote: "We exceedingly regret that it was necessary to have a legal execution in our county." He kept his coverage thorough but to the point as he attempted to "draw the mantle of forgetfulness about the horrors of the gallows."

Nevertheless, the hanging became an important part of Clarendon's history as the last and only judicial execution by hanging anywhere in the forty-six counties of the Texas Panhandle–South Plains region. Unlike its Wild West pioneer counterparts Tascosa and Mobeetee—now ghost towns— Clarendon remains a vibrant small town of two thousand souls. In 2004, the Clarendon Chamber of Commerce produced controversial T-shirts with a photo of the execution and the message, "I Hung Out in Clarendon."

Between 1819 and 1923, 390 people were hanged in Texas in the county where the trial took place, and four died by firing squad. Of these, 58 percent were Black, 25 percent White and 12 percent Hispanic. The races of the others are unknown.

Executions by hanging were terminated in 1923, when the State of Texas ordered all executions to be carried out by the state, in Huntsville, by means of the electric chair.

## DEBUNKING VIGILANTE VIOLENCE MYTHS OF THE TEXAS PLAINS

According to Western lore, many outlaws were "strung up" for stealing steeds and other misdeeds on the frontier. But mob violence and lynchings on the Texas plains were exceedingly rare. Most accounts of vigilante justice in the Panhandle–South Plains region are fables.

In the 1880s, the Texas Panhandle town of Tascosa in Oldham County was the quintessential Wild West setting for every sort of cowboy misconduct: gambling, womanizing, drunkenness, thievery and murder.

Henry W. McCullough was appointed Tascosa's city marshal in June 1882. A month later, McCullough attempted to arrest Frank Larqus for gambling. In the fracas that followed, "Mexican Frank" shot and killed the marshal.

A newspaper printed almost fourteen hundred miles away, the Wheeling, West Virginia *Daily Register*, published the following on July 29, 1882: "A Texas special says: At Gazasia, Oldham County, yesterday, Marion Frank, a mulatto, shot and killed Deputy Sheriff Henry McCullough. A large posse pursued the murderer, and he is reported caught and lynched."

However, Larqus—never known as Marion Frank and not a "mulatto"—was not lynched in the nonexistent town of "Gazasia" or elsewhere. The twenty-year-old tattooed gambler was convicted of McCullough's murder in September 1882 and sentenced to twenty-two years in prison. Larqus was pardoned in 1896 and released.

The most compelling Texas plains vigilante vengeance legend was in August 1888 in Palo Duro Canyon, Armstrong County. The only contemporary account of the event was published in several Illinois newspapers—one thousand miles from the Panhandle—on September 4, 1888. Each identical story was headlined: "Texas Vigilantes Exterminate a Band of Daring Outlaws."

The articles reported, "One of the most daring bands of outlaws that has existed in the west for years was wiped out of existence last Monday, near Paloduro, Armstrong county, Tex., by a band of vigilantes, in a pitched battle in which seventeen desperadoes and three vigilantes were killed."

The vigilantes surrounded the group of horse thieves and sent a demand to inspect what the thieves claimed were wild horses, according to the newspaper accounts. The desperadoes responded with a volley of gunfire, killing a man and two horses.

From every direction, the posse poured gunfire into the thieves' camp until there was silence. When the dust settled, seventeen horse thieves lay dead. The vigilantes suffered three dead and seventeen wounded. "An inspection of the dead proved that some of the most noted desperadoes of the border had at last met their deserts," according to newspaper stories.

The area was home to iconic cattleman Charles Goodnight in the 1880s, but Goodnight never mentioned the massacre in his memoirs. Indeed, no Armstrong County history volume tells the tale. Why would history forget the greatest gunfight of the West, which dwarfed the familiar tale of the Gunfight at the OK Corral? The newspaper story was probably a fabrication.

A third Texas Plains lynching is mentioned in a small footnote in the 2013 book *Forgotten Dead*. On April 26, 1886, in Lubbock County, "Unverified reports of the day claim that a Mexican man named Juan Telles [*sic*], suspected of having committed a murder, was dragged behind a horse and shot to death."

This misinterpreted tale probably originated from a newspaper article printed in the *Galveston Daily News* of May 10, 1886, about Juan Salles, who the previous Thursday had shot up Lubbock pioneer George Singer's store and set it afire. Salles died in the flames. There was no murder and no lynching, but after Salles died, cowboys "put a lariat around the Mexican, mounted their horses" and dragged him off to the plains.

The final unlikely Texas plains lynching was the subject of a short blurb in the 2015 book *Eternity at the End of a Rope*, about seven people lynched for murder in Castro County on April 30, 1897. Brief research reveals the lynching happened not in the South Plains County of Castro, but in Waller County, five hundred miles south.

One verified lynching occurred on the Texas frontier plains. The incident of December 29, 1887, resulted in the deaths of four members of the notorious Kelly family. They robbed and murdered at least eleven travelers who sought refuge at the Kelly tavern near the Kansas-Oklahoma border in "No Man's Land."

A posse of twenty relentlessly pursued the outlaws many miles south. Near Fort Elliott in Wheeler County, they tracked down fifty-five-year-old William Kelly, his wife, Kate, son Bill and daughter Kit. Kate fell from her horse in the chase, and her neck was broken. The vigilantes hanged William, Bill and Kit from the branch of a tree.

Perhaps other outlaws were strung up in the late nineteenth century on the plains of Texas, but none were reported. Prior to 1890, there were only three small towns in the forty-five-thousand-square-mile Panhandle–South Plains region. No more than twelve thousand souls populated the area. Few

Lynching of Kit Kelly, Wheeler County, 1887. *Public domain.*

lawmen and fewer newspapermen were available to document atrocities, but it seems the Kelly family incident is the only verified example of Texas plains frontier vengeance.

Unfortunately, lynching was widespread in more populous areas of the Lone Star State. Between 1885 and 1942, lynching was more common than legal execution in the state. At least 470 people were lynched during this period (466 were legally executed), including 339 Blacks (72 percent), 77 Whites (16 percent), 53 Hispanic (11 percent) and one Native American. Only Mississippi and Georgia recorded more lynchings than did Texas.

## LUBBOCK'S FIRST MURDER TRIAL: *STATE V. WILLIAM E. TAYLOR*

In 1892, Lubbock County citizens constructed the original county courthouse, located roughly in the same location as the current courthouse. The small wood-frame structure hosted little litigation until the arrival of the railroad in 1909, when Lubbock became a boomtown and was incorporated as a city. With the surge of activity, trouble followed, and the courthouse soon saw action.

Also in 1909, the newly incorporated City of Lubbock elected its first mayor, Frank E. Wheelock, a founding father of Lubbock County. Wheelock took his job seriously, insisting on strict law and order and instructing a city marshal to "shoot the belly off the first man that bothers you."

Another man under Wheelock's charge was William E. Taylor, destined to be the first person tried for murder in Lubbock.

On October 24, 1912, the weekly *Lubbock Avalanche* recounted sparse details of a shooting. Feedstore operator J.J. Reynolds and railroad grading contractor Tom Collins had been shot dead by three pistol shots the previous Saturday evening at the Blue Front Restaurant. The city's night watchman, Taylor, was arrested at the scene and released on bail. "The *Avalanche* does not deem it wise at this time to give the particulars of the sad affair as no trial has been had to date and it would not be best to give out the particulars now," the newspaper reported. "The affair is greatly regretted by everyone, and very little is being said about it one way or another."

But District Attorney J.E. Vickers knew the killings were the talk of the town. He was eager to win the first murder case to be tried in Lubbock County's new Seventy-Second District Court, created a year earlier. He quickly impaneled a grand jury.

Vickers's star eyewitness, "Big Ben" Borger, told grand jurors that the victims were unarmed and were felled by Taylor because they had laughed at the deputy marshal and would not be quiet. Collins bragged that he could take Taylor's gun, Borger testified.

Two murder indictments were handed down against Taylor. The case against Taylor for killing Collins was scheduled for trial first. Vickers prepared zealously, outlining compelling evidence. A miniature model of the Blue Front Restaurant—indicating locations of bodies and stray bullet holes—was constructed. Statements were reduced to typewritten memos. At least twenty-five state's witnesses were prepared to testify against Taylor.

Taylor's lawyer was William H. Bledsoe, who arrived in Lubbock in 1908, as had Vickers. Bledsoe argued self-defense, noting, "J.J. 'Jug' Reynolds had been arrested some 10 or 12 times and had numerous fights....'Poker Tom' Collins had beaten the Negro to death....Collins hit this town on the warpath.... Collins was drunk by 6 o'clock."

Twelve defense witnesses were subpoenaed, including influential names: Mayor Wheelock, Lubbock County sheriff W.H. Flynn and Coleman County sheriff W.L. Flitch.

The strength of the defense case did not escape Vickers. He scrambled to overcome Bledsoe's legal obstacles.

*State v. William E. Taylor* was tried in the creaky old Lubbock County Courthouse in early December 1912. Judge W.R. Spencer oversaw 108 prospective jurors and more than a week of trial proceedings.

On December 13, 1912, the *Avalanche* reported the verdict in the first murder trial in Lubbock's first district court on page twelve in subtle prose: "The trial of William E. Taylor for the killing of Thomas M. Collins in the Blue Front Restaurant in this City on the 19th day of October, which consumed last week, was given to the jury late Saturday afternoon. The jury after about three hours of deliberations, made known their desire to return a verdict, which was 'Not Guilty.'"

The report continued, "This was one of the most interesting cases which has been tried in Lubbock in many days and the Court Room was crowded at each session of Court, there being many women in attendance."

William H. Bledsoe.
*Courtesy Southwest Collection, Special Collections Library, Texas Tech University.*

Jurors and trial officials, *State vs. Taylor*, Lubbock, Texas, December 1912. *Courtesy Southwest Collection, Special Collections Library, Texas Tech University.*

After a change of venue, Taylor was to stand trial in Lynn County for the murder of J.J. Reynolds. When the prosecution appeared without witnesses, the judge dismissed the remaining indictment against Taylor, on September 3, 1913.

Taylor was never involved in law enforcement again. He farmed in the Lubbock area until his death in 1961.

Within three years, Lubbock's aging wood courthouse was replaced by a beautiful stone structure.

Bledsoe was elected state senator, championing the 1923 legislation that created Texas Technological College. He was a founding partner in the law firm now known as Crenshaw, Dupree & Milam.

Despite the pair of bitter defeats, Vickers established himself as a prominent trial lawyer and later as a district judge. He is remembered for advising young attorneys: "If the facts are against you, argue the law. If the law is against you, argue the facts. If both law and facts are against you, jump on the opposing lawyer."

Law practice has thus changed little in the past century.

# 3

# LOVE AFFAIRS AND LIQUOR LEAD TO MURDER

## THE PREACHER WHO POISONED HIS WIFE

On October 10, 1897, Methodist minister George E. Morrison faced his Sunday evening congregation and delivered a forceful—and prophetic—sermon, "The Wages of Sin Is Death!" in the tiny Carson County town known as Panhandle City, the setting for the deadly drama that would follow. As the services wound down with hymns, Reverend Morrison's wife, Minnie Morrison, lent her lilting soprano voice to the church choir.

Later that night, the preacher poisoned Minnie so he could marry his paramour.

George Edgar Morrison came from a respectable family. He was the son of A.B. Morrison, pastor of the Central Avenue Methodist Episcopal Church of Los Angeles. His sister Ada Morrison was a California postmaster.

Born in about 1858, George was described as handsome: five feet, nine inches tall with reddish-brown hair, a ruddy complexion and blue eyes. He was a gifted and charismatic orator. He might have been an actor or a politician, but he followed his father's example and chose to be a preacher.

He was educated at McKendree College in Illinois, where he met Annie Whittlesey. Romance blossomed, but for unknown reasons, the relationship ended.

After George's graduation, a Methodist bishop stationed the young preacher at a church in Hanford, California. There, he met Minnie Brady, a pretty, fair-haired, blue-eyed girl who sang in the church choir. Tragedy seemed to follow Minnie. When she was two, her mother was thrown from a horse and killed. Six months later, her father was trampled and killed by a runaway team of horses, and a year later, her brother was kicked in the head by a horse and died.

George and Minnie were married in 1880, and as was customary in Methodist ministries, the couple was bumped to churches around the country until they landed in Panhandle City on January 1, 1897.

George's job involved preaching two consecutive Sundays in Panhandle. Then, he would board a train and travel seventy-five miles north to preach in Canadian. From Canadian, he would ride another twenty-five miles north to Higgins, preach there the following Sunday and return home to Minnie.

Reverend George E. Morrison.
*Public domain.*

George was soon regarded as the most popular preacher in the community. But after seventeen years of marriage to Minnie, he strayed. In the late summer of 1897, he travelled to Topeka, Kansas, ostensibly to see a physician about a throat ailment. In Topeka, George looked up his former sweetheart, Annie, described as "a raven-haired beauty."

Annie's family was prominent, owners of a chain of grocery stores and an insurance company. They were devout Christian Scientists. George discovered that she possessed a substantial dowry, including $100,000 in cash, worth about $3 million in modern dollars. He told Annie he was single, a wealthy cattleman from Higgins. On a buggy ride, their romance was rekindled. He proposed. She accepted. But George said he needed time to make wedding arrangements and returned to Texas.

George and Annie exchanged dozens of letters. He used an address in Higgins to hide the steamy correspondence from his wife. He called Annie his "baby girlie" and "darling baby wife." In his letters to Annie, George concocted an elaborate diversion about a fictional cousin, the Reverend Guy E. Morrison, a Methodist minister in Panhandle City, married to Minnie.

Worried that Annie's family would not accept him, he produced letters of recommendation from Texas lawyers and deeds to vast ranches in the Panhandle. All were forgeries.

There was another obstacle to George's marriage to Annie. He was still married to Minnie.

In late September, George visited the local drugstore and bought ten cents worth of quinine, a common over-the-counter medication, usually sold in capsules. He insisted that the medication and capsules be separated in two bags, saying he preferred to fill the capsules himself.

On October 8, he obtained a quantity of the poison strychnine from the same pharmacist, explaining that varmints were bothering his chickens.

George learned that Panhandle City's only doctor was to take a month-long excursion, and he visited the depot to make sure the physician caught his train.

Following his fiery sermon that fateful Sunday evening, George and Minnie were joined by parishioners as they walked home. Minnie was sociable and in a good mood, but when they settled in for the evening, the preacher told his wife she looked a little under the weather. He insisted she take quinine and he inserted a capsule into a peach slice to mask the bitter taste. Minnie ate the strychnine-poisoned peach.

About ten o'clock, George summoned two neighbor ladies, saying his wife was ill. The neighbors witnessed Minnie in spasms, unable to speak, her hands tightly clenched, her arms drawn across her breast, her spine curved in a ball.

George said someone should fetch the local doctor, but he was informed the doctor was out of town. George raised his hands and cried, "My God, what will we do?"

As his wife seemed to fall asleep, George said she would be OK in the morning. The ladies left, and Minnie died just after midnight. She was forty-three. The preacher's wife was buried on October 12 at Panhandle.

George delayed notifying Minnie's family of her death, but he immediately wrote a letter to Annie describing the elaborate fictional funeral of Minnie, the wife of his nonexistent cousin, Reverend Guy E. Morrison. George took off for Topeka the day after Minnie's funeral.

The symptoms of Minnie's agonizing death were the talk of the town. Authorities exhumed her body and sent internal organs to a Galveston toxicologist for examination. The cause of death was disclosed: strychnine poisoning. Soon, the Reverend Morrison was a wanted man, charged with murder, a capital offense.

Kansas authorities acted on the Carson County warrant and found George with Annie. He was detained in Topeka, but Texas lawmen were slow to seek his extradition, and George was released. He left Annie and wandered about the West and Mexico under various aliases.

A mugshot drawing of his face was produced, and eleven thousand wanted posters were distributed across the country. Newspapers called him "The Most Diabolical Criminal in the History of Texas." In late November, George was spotted and apprehended in San Francisco. He was planning to join the navy and sail to Cuba.

George was transported to the Carson County Jail. His father and sister Ada arrived in Panhandle from California. They employed defense counsel for George: Temple Houston, youngest son of iconic Texas hero Sam Houston. He was the most celebrated lawyer of the frontier Texas plains.

Only four hundred souls populated Carson County in 1897, and everyone had an opinion about the case, so Houston's motion for change of venue was granted. George would stand trial in Vernon, Wilbarger County, 160 miles to the southeast. Trial began in September 1898, and the courtroom was packed with observers.

The prosecution produced a parade of witnesses from Panhandle: the druggist who sold the quinine and strychnine, the neighbor ladies who witnessed the symptoms of poisoning and the local doctor who told George he was leaving town. Temple Houston was confident he could beat the state's circumstantial evidence case. Minnie's death could have been a suicide! Or an accident!

But George's own written words were his doom. Annie testified for the prosecution and produced all of the preacher's love letters, making his web of deceit and motive to kill Minnie clear to the jury.

Houston offered depositions from a California physician and his wife. They recalled that Minnie had threatened suicide because of distress arising from "female derangement." Houston called George's sister Ada, who testified that Minnie "had been a sufferer from female trouble ever since she had arrived at the age of puberty. Minnie said death would be preferable to such suffering."

Temple Houston rested after presenting perhaps the least-inspired defense of his illustrious career. George was convicted of Minnie's murder and sentenced to die by hanging. All appeals failed.

Ada and a contingent of lawyers traveled to Austin to persuade Texas governor George Sayers to commute her brother's sentence to life imprisonment. As Sayers was considering the request, he received an urgent telegraph from Vernon. The message revealed that just three days before his scheduled execution, the preacher and two other inmates tried to break out of the Wilbarger County Jail. One of the prisoners attacked a guard serving food, and George yelled, "Kill the jailer!" The other two prisoners escaped, but George was captured.

Grave of Minnie Morrison. Her last name was misspelled, perhaps as a final rebuke to her husband. *Courtesy Squarehouse Museum.*

After hearing the news of the preacher's attempted escape, the governor sent a telegraph to Vernon: Morrison must die.

Wilbarger County sheriff J.T. Williams was concerned about another jailbreak. He asked W.S.J. Sullivan to travel to Vernon. The six-foot, six-inch former Texas Ranger was assigned to be George's cellmate and to keep a close watch on the prisoner until his execution.

On October 27, 1899, the preacher climbed the gallows in Vernon and faced a congregation of one thousand from all parts of Texas and beyond. He delivered a sort of sermon, saying it was difficult for man to discern night from morning, but that his God would stand ready to meet him. He denied his guilt, saying he would see his dear wife and mother on the other side. The Panhandle preacher said he held no malice against anyone.

As the sheriff adjusted the noose, George stood erect and motionless. He dropped through the trapdoor at 12:45 p.m. and was pronounced dead fifteen minutes later.

George's loyal sister Ada was emotionally exhausted and financially strapped, unable to arrange for her brother's body to be transported to California for family funeral services. Kindly Vernon residents donated money for George's burial and Ada's train ride home.

The final resting place for the Reverend George Morrison is a fenced grave site a few miles east of Vernon. There is no marker, no memorial for the man, no reminder of his fateful sermon, "The Wages of Sin Is Death!"

Minnie's pauper's grave in Panhandle deteriorated with time. Years after her death, Minnie's final resting place was transformed into a sort of shrine to her memory. In the 1920s, women of the community placed a shell-encrusted concrete slab over the gravesite. The shells symbolize a safe journey to the unknown shore of life beyond.

Minnie's last name on her headstone was misspelled "Morison," perhaps as a final rebuke to George E. Morrison, the most diabolical criminal in the history of Texas.

## The Saga of Slippery Sam Cates, Crosby County's Crafty Miscreant

Two shotgun blasts a hundred years ago rocked Crosbyton, exposing the tiny South Plains town as a cauldron of sexual promiscuity, leading to death, scandal and intrigue. Yet, the compelling Roaring Twenties tale of Sam Cates, at the center of the drama, seems to have been forgotten. Until now.

Samuel W. Cates was born to Maggie Cates and Samuel Absalom Cates in McKinney, Texas, in 1896. The fourth of eleven children, he completed eight years of school.

By 1915, Sam was nineteen years old and living in the tiny town of Crosbyton, Texas, populated by about eight hundred souls. He was rather small, five feet, eight inches tall and 135 pounds, with brown eyes. Gold crowns covered his two front teeth.

Sam worked for J.W. Burton. Born in Iowa in 1873, Joseph W. Burton was a prominent attorney who practiced law across the South Plains. J.W. and his wife, Metta Burton, born in 1874 in Illinois, were married in 1905.

In about 1917, J.W. hired young Sam as a clerk in his law office and as a chauffeur for Metta. Sam also boarded at the Burton home.

On Monday, March 8, 1920, Sam drove to Lubbock to pick up Metta, who had been hospitalized for a "mental and nervous" condition. When Sam and Metta returned to their Crosbyton home about 10:00 p.m., J.W. was waiting.

Jealous accusations flew, as Metta accused her husband of having an affair with her young niece, Florence Carlton, a houseguest. Sam had informed Metta that while she was away, J.W. and Flo had taken two excursions, one to Lubbock and one to Blanco Canyon, returning home each time after midnight. Sam said, "They might have found an opportunity for the gratification of any mutual desire they might have had."

Then, all hell broke loose.

Metta "was fighting and upbraiding" J.W., Sam said. J.W. accused Sam of spreading lies about Flo and the lawyer and told Sam he must leave his home the following morning. As Sam described the scene, an enraged J.W.—over six feet tall—suddenly attacked the smaller Sam and then backed Metta against a wall, violently beating and choking his wife.

Sam settled the dispute. He grabbed a shotgun and fired two blasts, the first hitting the lawyer's arm, a superficial wound. The second blast, to J.W.'s side, proved fatal.

Sam placed a pillow beneath the head of the dying lawyer and apologized. J.W. clung to life and remained conscious for hours, taking his last breath early Tuesday morning. He was forty-six years old.

Sam was arrested, jailed and charged with murder.

Metta almost immediately executed her will, leaving almost half of her estate to—Sam Cates! Within a few weeks, the widow was dead of natural causes. She was forty-five. Sam's inheritance amounted to about $7,000, worth $90,000 in today's dollars.

J.W. Burton's suspected romantic excursion to Blanco Canyon with his wife's niece spurred the violence that followed. *Photo by Ashton Thornhill.*

The scene of the 1920 murder on the back porch of the Crosbyton home of J.W. and Metta Burton. *Public domain.*

In May 1920—only three months after the shooting—the Crosby County Courthouse was the setting for Sam's trial. The indictment charged "murder with malice aforethought," a capital crime. If convicted, Sam faced the prospect of execution by hanging.

The prosecution alleged that Metta and Sam were involved in an illicit affair and conspired to murder the lawyer. Sam said he acted in self-defense and in defense of Metta.

The jury was told of Metta's generous bequest in favor of Sam. The jury also heard of Sam's intense interest—from jail—in whether Metta had executed her will before her death.

The twenty-three-year-old Sam testified and denied having had a sexual relationship with Metta. But in later court documents, he admitted that the couple had engaged in a torrid two-year love affair.

Sam "had access to the person of Mrs. Burton almost as unlimited and free as that of the deceased himself," according to court pleadings. "Such relations were invited by Mrs. Burton and took place not only in distant parts of the country, but also in the home of the deceased."

Despite the shameful revelations, J.W. and Metta Burton were buried side-by-side in an Iowa cemetery.

An eyewitness to the shooting was twenty-two-year-old Mary Steffen, the Burtons' maid and cook. Mary, who had worked for the Burtons since age sixteen, was another beneficiary of Metta's will. Mary, like Sam, was bestowed property valued at $90,000 in modern dollars. She was expected to be the prosecution's most important witness.

Instead, Mary testified for the defense, but whether she helped Sam's case is doubtful. She portrayed J.W. as the aggressor on the night of March 8, "jumping" on Sam and choking Metta. But she also described in explicit detail Sam's love affair with Metta, including liaisons she had witnessed in Texas, Iowa and Illinois. Mary's testimony may have sealed Sam's fate. She said that J.W. was on the ground—and not choking his wife—when the second, fatal shot was fired.

The prosecution made a "herculean effort" to obtain the death penalty. Sam dodged the hangman's noose but was convicted and sentenced to ninety-nine years in prison. He appealed.

The Texas Court of Criminal Appeals ruled that the evidence of Sam Cates's inheritance from J.W. Burton's wife was inadmissible. The matter was returned to Crosby County for a new trial, but the case was so notorious that an impartial jury could not be found. Lubbock County was chosen for a change of venue.

Meanwhile, Metta's bequests to Sam and Mary Steffen never materialized. Metta's sister contested the will, and many witnesses testified that Metta was of "unsound mind" when she executed the document. Affidavits described her "ranting and raving" following her husband's death. The judge agreed that the will was illegitimate, and Sam and Mary lost their claims to Metta's estate.

The *Crosbyton Review* and the *Lubbock Avalanche* published dramatic accounts of the second trial, in June 1921. Many witnesses were "taken through a close examination, and when the State would draw out several points in their favor, the counsel of the defendant would tear down the evidence until so to speak, they would break about even."

Metta's niece, Florence Carlton, a houseguest at the time of the shooting— and accused by the defense of having an affair with J.W.—testified that she heard no threats from the lawyer. She saw Sam fire both shots and saw J.W. lying on the ground when the second shot was fired.

Sam testified for five hours. "Answering in a very mild and polite tone of voice, and sometimes with a smile," he swore that J.W. attacked him and then attacked Metta. He said his first shot was not to kill, but to show that he meant business. Sam said he accidentally wounded J.W. in the arm. The lawyer did not fall but continued to choke his wife. J.W. cried, "Kill me, damn you!" Sam then shot to kill.

The prosecution subpoenaed Mary Steffen to repeat her vivid description of Sam and Metta's love affair and to testify that she saw a defenseless and wounded J.W. on the ground when Sam shot-gunned the lawyer to death.

However, in a bizarre but brilliant move, minutes before Mary was to take the witness stand, she and Sam were joined in matrimony in a civil ceremony at the courthouse. Mary's testimony harmful to Sam's case was never heard, barred by the marital privilege.

The legal-stunt marriage probably saved Sam from a much longer prison term. After a weeklong trial, the Lubbock jury convicted Sam and sentenced him to fourteen years in the Texas penitentiary.

Sam's lawyers took his case to the Court of Criminal Appeals a second time. But this time, his appeal did not get far, as Sam took an unauthorized leave of absence.

In August 1921, while housed at the Lubbock County Jail awaiting transfer to prison, Sam wrote a letter to a Dallas friend: "Listen, Clyde, we are in great need of some 'hack saws.' You get a half dozen, and pack them in a box of candy." Alas, a deputy intercepted the note, and no hacksaws were delivered to the jail.

A month later, Sam and two others attacked Lubbock County sheriff Charles Holcomb and his wife, Minnie Holcomb, as they served lunch to the prisoners. The inmates overpowered the sheriff, and Sam took his gun. "Throw up your hands! Put 'em up!" he yelled. As Sam held the gun on the sheriff, his accomplices attempted to gag his wife and choked her. Suddenly, Deputy Sheriff John McCulloch appeared and leveled his pistol on Sam.

The sheriff shouted, "Shoot him, John!" The deputy fired, but the bullet passed under Sam's arm. After the deputy missed, Sam sprang for the door. The sheriff tackled Sam and wrested the gun away. All prisoners were subdued.

When the dust settled, the inmates were locked away in the "dark cell," which the sheriff thought was escape-proof. As Sheriff Holcomb busied himself with a major chicken theft involving thirty-five hens and seven fryers, he was confident his prisoners were secure in his dungeon.

But the sheriff was wrong.

On September 30, 1921, Sam and an accomplice busted out of jail. Parts of their cots were strewn about the cell, and a small steel bar about the size of a pencil was also found. It was a mystery how the two broke out of the escape-proof dark cell.

Sam left a sarcastically tender parting note to Sheriff Holcomb: "Dear Charlie and Family, I hope you all the best of luck all the rest of your days.

Don't think too hard of me for doing this. I too am very sorry for our other troubles so please forgive me. If you people don't ever catch me, *you can bet that I will always be a good boy*. With love, always, Sam."

Sam and his accomplice went their separate ways after the jailbreak. Sam eventually surfaced in the remote desert town of Indio, California. Using the name John Lewis, he waited tables at a restaurant and made many friends in the small town of about one thousand residents.

The fugitive made the mistake of telling a friend that he was wanted by the law in Texas. Unfortunately for Sam, the remark reached the local sheriff's office, and he was arrested in January 1922.

On his recapture in California, Sam had $250 in the bank ($3,000 in current dollars), fine clothes and other valuable possessions. A letter signed by Indio's most prominent citizens attested to his excellent character. He had been in Indio less than four months. His employer said, "He was very faithful and honest with me," and asked to be informed of Sam's fate. He seemed always to be "a good boy" in Indio.

Sheriff Holcomb hurried to California to retrieve Sam, the man who had once held a gun on the sheriff and choked his wife. He was naturally curious how Sam had broken out of a supposedly inescapable dark cell. Sam was happy to boast of his intricate and complicated jailbreak. He used pieces of his cot to fashion tools to spring the cell's lock, reached open windows at the top of the jail, made a ladder of bed linens and swung to the ground.

Back in Lubbock for court, Sam had two years added to his penitentiary term, punishment for his assault of Sheriff Holcomb. The assault sentence was stacked atop the fourteen-year murder judgment, so he was sent to prison for a total of sixteen years.

Meanwhile, the Court of Criminal Appeals refused to hear Sam's appeal of his Lubbock County conviction, deciding that "the jurisdiction of the appellate court does not attach because of the escape pending appeal."

His prison release date was calculated: February 25, 1938, when Sam would be forty-two years old. Sam secretly set about to rearrange his release date. At first, he portrayed himself as a model prisoner.

Soon after arriving at an East Texas penitentiary in March 1922, he wrote to the *Avalanche* with a polite request for reading material for the prison library. The *Avalanche* promised to send a carload of books and magazines. But Sam had no plans for casual reading.

Within a year of writing his letter to the newspaper, Sam sawed through the bars of his cell window, stole a car and escaped. When he was recaptured, prison authorities ordered twenty lashes, but somehow the "punishment [was] set aside and lost [good] time restored," according to penitentiary records.

In 1926, after having served only four years of his sixteen-year sentence, Sam was pardoned by Texas governor Miriam "Ma" Ferguson and released from prison. Governor Ferguson—who granted more than four thousand pardons during a four-year period—was rumored to have granted many of the reprieves in exchange for cash payments. Most of Ma's pardons were for those convicted of liquor-related crimes during Prohibition. As Sam was not a bootlegger and apparently had little money, it is a mystery why he was favored by the governor's pardon.

Some fourteen years later, census records show that Sam was living in Harris County, employed as a cook at a downtown restaurant. He was listed as divorced, and there is no record he ever fathered children. He registered for the World War II draft in 1942, and that is the last we know of Sam Cates.

Mary Steffen—the girl Sam wed just before she was to testify against him—seems to have disappeared after her name was listed in the 1920 census as a "servant" in the Burton home. Records indicate she never remarried and may have been buried in Wisconsin in 1966 at age sixty-six or sixty-seven.

Sam died in 1984 at age eighty-seven and was buried in Parker County, Texas.

It seems "Slippery" Sam Cates, Crosby County's crafty miscreant, was "always a good boy" after his pardon by Governor Ferguson. He had no more run-ins with the law and made no more daring escapes.

It remains a mystery how Sam—mostly—got away with it all.

## MURDER ON THE COURTHOUSE STEPS: THE PAYNE-RIPPY FEUD

According to legend, the Payne-Rippy feud started over a poker game in Dimmit, Texas. The feud more likely arose when South Plains farmers got involved in bootleg whiskey trafficking during Prohibition. How it truly began remains a mystery, but the feud came to a bloody climax on the steps of the Crosby County Courthouse on May 14, 1923.

Of the four main characters involved, James Sweazea seemed least likely to become entangled in controversy. Sweazea was a pioneer Castro County farmer who settled there in 1898. By the beginning of the feud in

1922, he was a seventy-two-year-old retired widower, having raised nine children. He owned a new Buick touring car, an important element in the upcoming drama.

Sweazea became acquainted with Maud Rippy, a Castro County farmer. Married with two children, Maud was twenty-nine years old in 1922. He was tall with blue eyes and light-brown hair.

Rippy's brother Richard Rippy, known as Dick, was thirty-three when the feud began, with a wife and three kids. He was a Crosby County farmer who sold moonshine whiskey to the locals. Dick was tall and stout, with brown eyes and light-brown hair. Collectively, the Rippy brothers and Sweazea became known as the "Gang of Three."

On the opposite side of the feud was yet another farmer, David Leonard Payne. Payne's nickname, "Poppin," described his expertise with a gun. When the feud began, he was forty-seven and married with four children. Poppin was slight at five feet, five inches in height, with dark hair and blue eyes. He farmed in Crosby County, and his neighbor Dick Rippy helped him quench his thirst for illegal liquor.

The unverified gambling legend is compelling. It seems the Gang of Three and Poppin Payne were involved in a poker game in Dimmitt early in 1922. Poppin won everyone's money. When he left the table gloating, the Gang of Three beat Poppin with chairs until they thought he was dead. They called an undertaker, who was surprised to find Poppin clinging to life, and Poppin recovered from his wounds. It was the first of Poppin's multiple brushes with death.

Another explanation for the feud is more credible. Authorities discovered that Dick Rippy supplied "white mule"—moonshine—to Poppin, and they closed in. Dick was indicted for the felony crime of selling "liquors capable of producing intoxication." Poppin was to be the prosecution's star witness against Dick, who feared he would be sent to prison.

Dick invited his brother Maud to Crosby County for assistance. Maud was afraid his old jalopy would not make the one-hundred-mile trip from Dimmitt, so he recruited Swaezea to drive him in the old man's new Buick.

Violence soon erupted in the tiny Crosby County town of Ralls. Poppin's account—with no poker story—appeared in the *Crosbyton Review*:

> *I had been buying white mule from that bootlegger gang now and then when my son told them not to sell me anymore. They had some words over it and a few days later I was asked to go out to the home of a friend to look at a span of mules. I had supper with him and right after supper four men whom I*

*knew came up and without a word of warning one of them hit me over the head from the back with a chair and they all beat me up and left me. Two weeks ago [March 31, 1922], a man who had always been my friend took supper with me and we walked to town to look at a horse after supper. He stopped me in front of the barber shop which was dark and stepped to one side when someone opened fire on me with a shot gun. Three men were bound over on a $500 bond each for this shooting. Thirty-six pieces of lead were taken out of my legs and hips at that time at the Lubbock Sanitarium. Two days ago, I was discharged and Friday afternoon [April 14, 1922] I was working in my garden with my wife when a heavily curtained Buick passed the house slowly. A few minutes later it returned and drove right up to the fence. I saw them drop the curtain and start to shooting. They used two shot guns. The first shot knocked me down....Four times I tried to get up to run and each time they shot me down again. Then they drove away, and I ran into the house but gave out and had to be put to bed.*

Poppin—peppered from head to toe with buckshot—was hospitalized, and again he recovered. Meanwhile, lawmen in Lamb County spotted and stopped the Buick. Inside were the Rippys and Sweazea, two shotguns, two rifles and two pistols. The three men were arrested and soon indicted for two assaults with intent to murder Poppin. Investigators identified the Rippy brothers as the shotgunners and Sweazea as the driver in the "garden shooting."

Trial for the Gang of Three—indicted for two attempts to kill Poppin Payne—was scheduled for May 14, 1923, exactly thirteen months after the shotgun attack on Poppin in his garden. During a recess in the proceedings, defendants Maud Rippy and James Sweazea sat on the east steps of the Crosby County Courthouse discussing the case with their attorney.

Suddenly, Poppin appeared and emptied his six-shooter, killing Maud and Sweazea instantly. The third defendant, Dick Rippy, survived by locking himself in the courthouse men's room until the coast was clear. Poppin immediately surrendered to the sheriff. He was carrying two guns, a .45-caliber revolver and a .32-caliber automatic, one in each hand. Poppin handed the weapons to the sheriff, saying, "Put two marks on that big gun."

He was held in the more secure Lubbock County Jail and was soon indicted for the murders of Maud and Sweazea. According to the *Tulia Herald*, Payne "did not know Rippy and Sweaza were near when he left the courthouse. He states when he first saw Rippy, the latter was attempting to draw a gun and he...pulled his pistol and shot Rippy once, then shot Sweaza, turned and

The Crosby County Courthouse, site of the killings of Maud Rippy and James Sweazea, 1923. *Author's collection.*

shot Rippy again and then shot Sweaza again. He claims the two men have antagonized him for testifying against them in liquor cases."

But Poppin's victims were not armed. The case was transferred to Randall County on a change of venue, and proceedings began three months later. The courtroom was packed with spectators from each side of the feud, and extra protection was ordered by the judge. Texas Ranger Frank Hamer—later known for ambushing and killing Bonnie and Clyde—headed the security team. The atmosphere was tense.

On the second day of the trial, just after lunch, loud blasts were heard outside the courthouse. Spectators ducked for cover under courtroom furniture as others escaped through open windows. A short investigation revealed that someone had tried to start a Model T Ford, and the old tin lizzie backfired three or four times. After a thirty-minute recess, the trial resumed.

More than 250 witnesses were subpoenaed for Poppin's trial, and 41 testified. Prosecutors called for a life sentence, telling the jurors they would "not be doing their duty" if they set Poppin free. Poppin's lawyers argued for an acquittal based on self-defense, emphasizing details of the feud and the three attempts on Poppin's life.

On August 19, after the jury had deliberated more than sixteen hours, Poppin was found guilty of manslaughter and sentenced to five years in prison. Poppin appealed his conviction to the Texas Court of Criminal Appeals, complaining that the trial court had allowed Dick Rippy and others to testify to many of Poppin's irrelevant bad deeds. The appeals court's opinion, dated May 20, 1925, is vague about the specifics of the testimony, describing the evidence as "disconnected transactions and incidents in which appellant had assaulted and abused other persons…to indicate that he was generally a bad and dangerous man."

The appeals court reversed Poppin's conviction and ordered a retrial, instructing the trial court not to allow evidence of Poppin's extraneous misdeeds or details of the Payne-Rippy feud prior to the courthouse shootings.

Poppin's retrial was moved again, this time to Potter County, where the jury found him guilty of the lesser offense of assault with intent to murder Sweazea and sentenced him to two years in prison. Appeals failed. Venue was transferred to Lamb County for Poppin's trial for the murder of Maud Rippy. However, a plea deal was struck, and Poppin pled guilty to manslaughter, settling for a two-year prison sentence to run concurrently with his Potter County conviction.

Meanwhile, Poppin was briefly committed to the state insane asylum. He arrived at the Texas penitentiary at Huntsville on May 23, 1928, to serve simultaneous two-year sentences for assault with intent to murder and manslaughter. Eight months later, he escaped and remained free for more than two years. Nothing is known of his vacation from prison. He surrendered voluntarily on April 9, 1931, and discharged his sentences on December 15, 1931. Poppin died of natural causes less than a year later and was buried in Huntsville. He was fifty-eight years old, survived by his widow and six of their seven children.

The last member of the Gang of Three, Dick Rippy, was never tried for his involvement in the Payne-Rippy feud. His two indictments for assault with intent to murder and his bootlegging indictment were transferred to Floyd County on a change of venue. The cases were all dismissed in 1927 because Poppin—the main witness for the prosecution—was in the insane asylum at the time of Dick's trial. Dick fathered nine children and lived to age seventy. He was buried in Whittier, California.

## LUBBOCK'S FIRST EXECUTION: A LOVE AFFAIR GONE WRONG

Texas' long history of state-sponsored executions began in 1819, when, during Spanish rule, George William Brown was hanged for piracy at Galveston. Many years passed before a condemned man would be executed for a Lubbock County crime.

Before 1954, at least one Lubbock defendant was sentenced to death, but no executions took place due to successful appeals and clemency. In 1934, a Dickens County case was tried in Lubbock County after a change of venue. Virgil Stalcup was convicted of the murder of Dickens County sheriff W.B. Arthur. He was electrocuted at Huntsville in 1936.

Almost two decades passed before the ultimate punishment would be exacted on a Lubbock County offender. Events beginning in early January 1953 dominated Lubbock news headlines for months. Joyce Fern White, eighteen, was reported missing by her mother on January 7. Her boyfriend, Walter E. Whitaker Jr., joined in a fruitless search for the girl, suggesting she may have run away to San Antonio.

Walter, from a wealthy Connecticut family, was a twenty-year-old airman at Lubbock's Reese Air Force Base. Later, his court testimony provided details of their relationship and her tragic death. He met Joyce at Lawson's Roller-Skating Rink in August 1952. Romance blossomed, and by January 1953, the couple was discussing marriage.

Walter was notified of his transfer to San Antonio as a flying cadet. On January 6, he went to bid goodbye to Joyce. The girl insisted the two should marry, but he refused. Then, Joyce informed Walter she was with child. Convinced of her pregnancy, he agreed to immediately take her to Clovis, New Mexico, to marry. On the way, they stopped to make love. Afterward, she informed him she was not pregnant, and an argument ensued about his relationship with a former girlfriend.

Walter said Joyce slapped him, and the next thing he remembered was looking down and seeing her discolored face. Joyce was dead.

Eventually, he was questioned by police. After requesting counsel from a Lutheran minister, Walter led officers to the spot where he buried the girl's body. "He took a shovel and dug six different holes, five of which produced the clothing...and finally...he dug down about four to six feet and there they found the body of Joyce Fern," according to court documents.

Walter was indicted for "murder with malice," a capital crime, and the ensuing legal drama was unprecedented in Lubbock's history. Relentless media coverage was highly prejudicial against Walter, and the case was transferred to Wilbarger County on a change of venue.

Judge Vic Lindsey, known for his fairness and knowledge of the law, presided from the bench. Talented lawyers now considered icons of the Lubbock bar lined up on opposite sides of the case. The Lubbock County district attorney was thirty-two-year-old Travis Shelton, later president of the State Bar of Texas and a member of the Texas Criminal Defense Lawyers Association Hall of Fame. He was assisted by special prosecutor George W. Dupree, founding partner of the venerable Lubbock law firm Crenshaw, Dupree & Milam.

Another prosecutor was Assistant DA Forrest Bowers, later known as the dean of West Texas trial lawyers and honored by *Texas Lawyer* magazine in 2013 as one of the one hundred legal legends of the past one hundred years. The defense was anchored by former Lubbock County DA Burton Burks, assisted by Clifford Brown, later president of the Texas Criminal Defense Lawyers Association and a founder of the Lubbock Criminal Defense Lawyers Association.

Despite the change of venue and the notable lawyers involved, the trial assumed a circus atmosphere. Photographers captured dramatic events in and out of the courtroom, and the defendant, Walter, seemed to relish the publicity. Three days of jury selection produced twelve male jurors.

Walter testified, claiming what amounted to an "amnesia" defense. It did not work. The prosecution proved that he purchased cotton cord shortly

Assistant Lubbock County DA Forrest Bowers (*left*) and DA Travis Shelton, circa 1953. *Author's collection.*

before Joyce's death, and blood-stained cord was found with her corpse. Joyce had been strangled.

Following three days of testimony, jurors convicted Walter on June 27. His sentence was death. All appeals were rejected, and he was electrocuted at Huntsville on September 1, 1954.

Under modern legal standards, Walter's death sentence would be unlikely. No special circumstances were alleged, such as murder during a kidnapping or aggravated robbery. There was no bifurcation, meaning separate trials for guilt-innocence and punishment. And there was no showing that Walter was likely to commit future crimes of violence.

No other Lubbock County offender died in Huntsville's electric chair—"Old Sparky"—Texas's official execution method from 1924 to 1964. Prior to 1924, Texas executions were conducted in the county of conviction—usually by public hanging—and there is no record of a Lubbock County hanging or other form of execution prior to Walter Whitaker's 1954 electrocution.

Eight Lubbock County murderers—all men—were executed by lethal injection between 2000 and 2018.

# 4

# BIGGEST SOUTH PLAINS TRIALS OF THE TWENTIETH CENTURY

## LACH CASE AMONG LUBBOCK'S MOST NOTORIOUS MURDERS

The body of Sarah Morgan was found in a blood-spattered laboratory on the third floor of the Texas Tech University's Science Building on December 3, 1967. Sarah, a fifty-four-year-old Tech custodian, was found with her throat slashed by a scalpel. Her head was nearly decapitated by a bone saw. Her grandmaster custodial keys were missing.

The gruesome discovery was the beginning of one of the most notorious murder cases in Lubbock's history.

Local police, with practically no clues as to the identity of the "Scalpel Killer," began their search for what one official labeled a "thrill slayer." Lubbock and the Tech community were alarmed.

Months later, Tech professor Kent Rylander noticed that papers in his office had been disturbed, and he thought someone had broken into his office to obtain the answers for an exam he planned to administer the next day.

On March 13, 1968, Detectives Frank Wiley and Floyd Hargrave spent all night staked out in Rylander's office, on the third floor of the Science Building. Early that morning, a man opened the locked door to the office using Sarah's grandmaster key.

The detectives tried to arrest him, but he ran. A wild movie-style chase ensued. As police closed in, the man stole a parked car from campus. He ditched the car and sped off in another, reaching speeds of over one hundred miles per hour, but he was ultimately arrested by police.

The man was Benjamin Lach, a twenty-three-year-old Tech graduate student. Investigators believed he snuck into the building the previous December to steal test answers. Sarah caught him in the act, and he killed her.

Benjamin was soon indicted for "murder with malice"—a capital offense—and his case was eventually moved to Fort Worth on a change of venue. The case was tried in November 1970, with Tarrant County district judge Byron Matthews presiding.

Lubbock prosecutors Blair Cherry Jr. and Alton Griffin presented Benjamin's confession to the jury panel of eleven men and one woman. "I caught her from behind," Benjamin's written statement to police began. "I think I strangled her. She fell to the floor and then I don't remember what happened." The confession continued: "I decided to cut her up. I looked around and saw a scalpel." When he saw Sarah was dead, he grabbed her keys.

Several witnesses testified that they saw Benjamin in the building about 7:00 p.m. on the night of the murder.

Benjamin, represented by Lubbock lawyers Bill Gillespie and A.W. "Shorty" Salyars, relied on an alibi defense and contested the confession. Joan Dominick testified that she was with Benjamin at 8:00 p.m., the time of the murder. She said she met him by chance at the Student Union Building. He was with her between 6:30 p.m. and 9:00 p.m., she said.

A Dallas psychologist testified that Benjamin was a paranoid schizophrenic and suggested he could have been pressured into making a confession that he killed Sarah, even if he were innocent.

The defense called Benjamin's mother to the stand. Mrs. Herman Lach, of Boston, wept quietly during her testimony. She portrayed her life in Europe as a Jew during World War II and the extermination of many members of her family by Nazis.

She said her son was born in Poland and described the family journey to the United States after the war, as well as Benjamin's upbringing. She traced Benjamin's education and background, pointing out his participation in football, tennis, bowling, swimming and Red Cross lifesaving. Benjamin also served as a summer camp counselor, she said.

The defense also introduced a December 1968 Lubbock court decree that found Benjamin insane (incompetent to stand trial, in today's legal terminology).

In final arguments, prosecutor Griffin argued, "Sarah Morgan gave her life, so Benjamin Lach could make good grades."

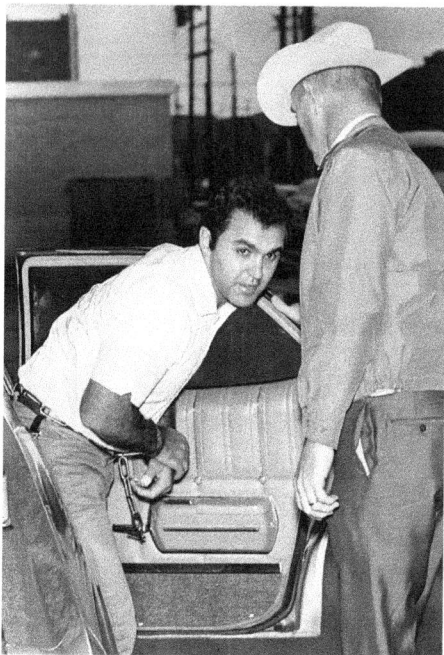

Benjamin Lach at the time of his arrest, March 13, 1968. *Courtesy* Lubbock Avalanche-Journal.

As the jury deliberated, Benjamin's mother told the press, "In some countries, there is no justice. I hope there is justice in this country. But I wait to see. My son is innocent. He told me." The jury deliberated two hours before convicting Benjamin. Though the prosecution sought the death penalty, Cherry and Griffin presented no evidence at the punishment phase of the trial. The jury sent Benjamin to prison for forty years.

After serving fifteen years and seven months of his sentence, Benjamin was paroled in 1983. Texas law allowed Benjamin to be released early, because the college degrees he earned in prison counted toward time served.

Benjamin is believed to be living in Massachusetts.

There is a story—perhaps fictional—about prosecutor Cherry and defense lawyer Salyars following the trial. At a bar association meeting, Cherry complimented his friend Salyers, "If I were ever in trouble with the law, I would want Shorty Salyars to defend me." In response, Salyars grinned and said, "If I were ever in trouble with the law, I would want Blair Cherry to prosecute me!"

# LYNN COUNTY CASE AMONG LAST CAPITAL RAPE EXECUTIONS

Today, the Redwine community is absorbed by cotton fields. But in the 1960s, it marked the junction of two lonely county roads in southeast Lynn County, on the pancake-flat South Plains of Texas. A young farmer, Fred Thompson (pseudonym), established his cotton operations near Redwine in the late 1950s.

He and his twenty-seven-year-old wife, Mary (pseudonym), were the parents of an eight-year-old son and an eleven-month-old daughter. They lived in a tiny *L*-shaped frame farmhouse with just two bedrooms and a bath, a kitchen and a living room. Their closest neighbor lived a mile away.

The following is what Mary later told a Lynn County jury. There was a knock on her door on the afternoon of April 25, 1961. Her husband had gone to Lubbock and her son was at school. She was alone with the baby. When she answered the door, a big "colored" man forced his way in, grabbed her by the throat and raped her repeatedly. Afterward, he apologized and asked her to get a gun and kill him.

"No, I'm not going to kill you," Mary replied. "You didn't kill me. I'm going to pray for you." The man then drove away in a blue pickup.

As soon as the pickup was gone, Mary rushed about the house gathering diapers, milk bottles and the baby. She jumped into the family car and sped away. But five miles down the road, she spotted the rapist's pickup in the distance. She ducked into the A.G. Huffaker farmstead and rushed screaming with her baby girl into the house.

No one was home. Mary crawled into a closet in a rear bedroom and closed the door. She cowered there with her baby until she heard footsteps on the hardwood floors. Panic gave way to composure as she realized the light footsteps were not those of a two-hundred-pound man.

Mary emerged and announced herself to Ms. Huffaker. She had Ms. Huffaker lock all the doors and grabbed the telephone. Mary called several places and finally found Fred, who hurried to his wife's rescue.

Fred took her to a physician in Post, where she was treated and released. There is no evidence Fred, Mary or the physician ever called law enforcement. Ms. Huffaker did not call law enforcement either. Nor did she ever testify. Fred Thompson never testified. The physician who treated Mary did not testify.

The same afternoon, Lynn County deputy Elton Corley was flagged down by a young Black man on the roadway: his name was Bennie Lee McIntyre.

Bennie told the deputy he had seen a "colored man" who was dressed just like him coming from the Thompson home.

Bennie came to the South Plains in late 1960 from the small town of Rosebud, in Falls County, almost four hundred miles east of Lynn County. When he reached Lynn County, Bennie was eighteen years old, just under six feet tall and almost 230 pounds. He worked as a farm laborer and lived in a barracks building near Grassland, a crossroads village just six miles northeast of the Redwine community.

Sheriff Booger Redwine soon arrived and spoke with Bennie for a moment. Then Corley followed the sheriff's car, with Bennie in the passenger seat, to the Thompson home. No one was there, but it was apparent something may have happened, as furniture was askew.

The district attorney of the multicounty district, George Hansard, was headquartered in Lamesa, thirty-two miles to the south, and that was the sheriff's next stop. In Lamesa, Bennie gave a statement to the DA, but that statement was never produced at trial nor provided to the defense.

Two days later, on April 27, Bennie was taken to the Texas Department of Public Safety office in Lubbock. There, he was read his Miranda warnings. He gave Lynn County attorney Harold Green a second statement, a rambling, three-page confession to the rape of Mary Thompson.

Bennie said he had gone to three or four farmhouses with the idea of raping a white woman. "I wanted to do that with a white woman for two or three years," the statement read. "I know it is wrong, and against the law. I know I would be punished for that."

No one in Lynn County could remember a similar crime having ever been committed in the sleepy South Plains farming community. Reaction was swift and hot, especially among members of the close-knit hamlet of Grassland, just a few turnrows from the Redwine community. The two hundred citizens of Grassland supported three churches.

On the night of the offense, a Black man was burned in effigy. Some reported that the event happened in Grassland; others said Grasslanders staged the demonstration on the courthouse lawn in Tahoka, the county seat. There was an ugly incident at the Grassland grocery store. Someone ordered the proprietor not to serve a Black woman if he wanted to stay in business.

The same night, Tahoka police chief Jack Miller was approached on the courthouse square by two Grassland men, "Preacher" Leach and Alton Greer. Leach was the minister of Central Baptist Church, and Greer was a relative of Mary Thompson. They demanded to know the location of "the Negro." It was their unspoken intention—and that of dozens of other enraged Grassland residents present—to string him up. Leach and Greer led an attempt to get into the courthouse before being turned back.

But the lynch mob would not have found Bennie in the courthouse jail. Sheriff Redwine, who witnessed the incident, had already taken steps to protect the accused from the mob. Instead of housing him in one of the three small cells of the third-floor Lynn County Courthouse jail, the sheriff moved the prisoner to the Lubbock County Jail, thirty miles north. In his ten years as sheriff, Redwine had not found it necessary to take such precautions to protect a prisoner. The sheriff did not investigate the incidents in Grassland or the attempted lynching.

Bennie was indicted by the Lynn County grand jury on May 3, eight days following the crime. The document accused him of "unlawfully, in and upon Mary Thompson, a woman, did make an assault; and did then and there by force, threats, and fraud, and without the consent of the said Mary Thompson, ravish and have carnal knowledge of the said Mary Thompson." It was a capital crime.

Only a handful of lawyers practiced in the four small counties of the 106th Judicial District. Mitchell Williams of Tahoka, the former district attorney, was appointed to represent Bennie the same day he was indicted. The following day, Lamesa lawyer John Saleh was assigned as co-counsel.

The Lynn County Courthouse, site of the capital rape trial of Bennie Lee McIntyre, 1961. *Author's collection.*

District Judge Truett Smith, also a former district attorney, scheduled Bennie's trial for May 15 at the Lynn County Courthouse in Tahoka. The defense objected to the rush to justice and urged the judge to move the trial away from the simmering public indignation that seemed to permeate Lynn County.

Meanwhile, Saleh and Williams located Bennie's relatives in distant Falls County for information that might be useful in the young man's defense. They contacted a Lubbock neuropsychiatrist, Dr. Jerome A. Smith, and arranged a sanity examination of Bennie.

On May 11, District Attorney Hansard gave the defense lawyers a list of the state's witnesses. Aside from a copy of the indictment, the witness list was the only discovery provided by the prosecution.

Court proceedings began exactly twenty days following the rape of Mary Thompson. Preliminary matters were heard Monday, May 15, as Saleh litigated the motion for change of venue and motion for continuance, still awaiting a report from the psychiatrist. He called several witnesses in support of the defense motions.

Without asking for legal argument, the judge denied all defense motions, and the case proceeded to jury selection on Tuesday. Individual jury selection lasted three days, and testimony was set to begin Friday morning, May 19.

Well before the courthouse opened for business that Friday morning, a crowd began to gather. People meandered about the expansive public lawn, perched on the steep steps to the north and south courthouse entrances and huddled in the hallways. When the courtroom opened, they rushed in and claimed their places.

The Lynn County Courthouse was built in 1916, and seating was limited to 178 oak theater-style chairs. In addition, there was a balcony reminiscent of *To Kill a Mockingbird*, but the balcony apparently was not consigned to African Americans. Spectators brought sack lunches so they would not lose their seats during the noon recess. Those who could not find a seat lined the walls of the courtroom. The gallery included a "good number of Negroes," and "two or three Mexicans," Sheriff Redwine observed. No one had ever seen such a crowd at the Lynn County Courthouse.

The temperature that day would reach eighty-eight degrees, but county officials had air-conditioning installed especially for the McIntyre trial.

About 9:00 a.m., the trial began with a jolt. John Saleh stood and announced, "May it please the Court, and Ladies and Gentlemen of the Jury and Prosecution, at this time the defendant pleads guilty to the indictment and throws himself on the mercy of the Court and the Jury."

Judge Smith admonished Bennie that his plea of guilty could result in a death sentence. "Do you persist in your plea of guilty?"

"Yes, sir," Bennie replied. And his trial began.

There were no opening statements. The state called Mary to tearfully recount her story and identify Bennie as her attacker. There was no cross-examination. Deputy Corley and Sheriff Redwine briefly described their encounters with Bennie. There was no cross-examination. Finally, County Attorney Green presented Bennie's confession. The state rested its case.

For the defense, Saleh presented three witnesses. Sheriff Redwine testified that Bennie had no criminal record. Bennie's uncle and mother told the jury about his short life, growing up in poverty and without education in a single-parent home, forced to provide for his mother and three younger brothers.

The evidence was concluded.

The state's argument included Green telling the jury that a verdict of death "would serve to deter other colored men. It will be made known to all who are like inclined as Bennie Lee McIntyre…to do this to a white lady. They will know."

The bulk of the defense's final argument is illustrated by this statement from defense counsel Mitchel Williams: "I am not sure that I know now what I am going to say. I have been in this case as Court appointed counsel.…I have searched my conscience.…I do not condone rape.…I am sorry.…I have not envied my position in this case."

The jury returned with its verdict in just over an hour and a half: "We, the jury, find the defendant guilty as charged in the indictment and assess his punishment at death."

Bennie turned to his lawyers and thanked them. The trial ended before 6:00 p.m. on the day it began, twenty-two days following the rape in Redwine.

Saleh and Williams's appeal to the Texas Court of Criminal Appeals was rejected, and their writ of certiorari to the United States Supreme Court was refused.

Bennie was executed at Huntsville on January 20, 1963, less than three years following the rape in Redwine. He was twenty-one years old.

Judge Smith ordered Lynn County to pay defense lawyers Williams and Saleh for their services on behalf of the defendant. The check was $125, which the lawyers refused to cash.

Bennie was among the last eight men to die in "Old Sparky," and one of the youngest. Only two convicted rapists were executed following Bennie Lee McIntyre.

In 1964, only a year after the McIntyre electrocution, legal challenges to capital punishment resulted in a de facto moratorium on executions in the United States. In 1972, the United States Supreme Court examined Georgia's "unitary trial" procedure (in which the jury was asked to return a verdict of guilt or innocence and, simultaneously, determine whether the defendant would be punished by death or life imprisonment.) The high court held Georgia's death penalty procedure to be unconstitutional on the grounds that it was a cruel and unusual punishment in violation of the Eighth Amendment to the United States Constitution. This essentially negated all death penalty sentences nationwide.

At the time of the decision, fifty-two Texas inmates were awaiting execution; all were commuted to life in prison by Texas governor Preston Smith of Lubbock. The decision led to a 1973 revision of Texas laws, primarily by introducing the bifurcated trial process and narrowly limiting the legal definition of capital crimes. Rape, for example, was no longer a capital offense.

# Homer Maxey's Lawsuit:
## Lubbock's Longest and Largest

Lubbock's population exploded between 1930 and 1970, jumping from 20,000 to almost 150,000 residents. To accommodate the growth, new homes and commercial property were desperately needed. Homer Maxey rose to the challenge but in the process spurred the longest and most bitter civil lawsuit in Lubbock's history.

Maxey's father was a Lubbock contractor, so, in 1924, at age thirteen, Maxey's first job was helping erect a building at the new college, Texas Tech.

Maxey worked his way through Tech as a janitor. After graduation, he cofounded Maxey Lumber Company. The same year, he started developing real estate, including Federal Housing Administration properties such as Maxey Place and Melba Addition.

Meanwhile, Maxey married his high school sweetheart, Melba Tatom. Daughters Carla Maxey and Glenna Maxey came along in the late 1930s.

World War II interrupted Maxey's career. He accepted a commission in the navy in 1942 and valiantly commanded large landing craft in Pacific naval battles.

After his return, in 1946, he founded Homer G. Maxey & Company, a wholesale plumbing and electrical supply firm. He was one of the first

Homer Maxey. *Courtesy Maxey family and Broadus Spivey.*

South Plains developers of suburban retail shopping centers, such as the Plaza Shopping Center. Other projects quickly followed: the Plaza Apartments, the Lubbock Apartments, Modern Manor, the downtown Veteran's Administration Building, the Plainsman Hotel.

Maxey became a millionaire by the mid-1950s.

As he expanded his businesses and construction projects and ventured into ranching, Maxey relied on the advice of a Lubbock law firm, Evans, Pharr, Trout & Jones. He and attorney Bill Evans of the firm partnered in a new project: the renovation and expansion of the Pioneer Hotel.

Evans's firm also represented Citizens National Bank, the oldest bank in Lubbock. On advice of his attorneys, Maxey eventually encumbered almost the entirety of his assets to Citizens to fund building projects and investments, including a risky cattle operation. The bank's president was E.W. Williams Jr.

By 1965, the law firm and the bank had relocated to the new Citizens Tower, an eleven-story downtown showplace. Chauncey Trout and Charlie Jones, partners in the law firm, were named to the board of directors of the bank.

Suddenly, on February 16, 1966, the bank in a secret meeting at the bank foreclosed on Homer Maxey. Plaza Building Corporation, which owned most of the ranchland, stock in several of Maxey's businesses, his home and other assets, was sold for $749 to Monterey Lubbock Corporation, a subsidiary of Citizens. All of his other property was sold under similar circumstances that afternoon. Trout and Jones were involved on behalf of the bank.

Bank president Williams said later: "It doesn't sound good, but it was legal." It destroyed Maxey's financial existence. He was totally broke, and he was also homeless. Maxey sued the bank, his lawyers, Monterey Lubbock Corp., Williams and many others. More than two dozen of Lubbock's richest and most influential citizens were named as defendants.

In many ways, the case boiled down to an argument about which side was correct on the math. According to Maxey's appraisals, he was worth $5.5 million at the time of the foreclosure and owed the bank less than $2 million.

71

But aside from recovering his millions, Maxey wanted to show betrayal and unethical behavior as themes, and he wanted his reputation back.

The 1969 trial lasted three months—still the longest jury trial in Lubbock's history—and was front-page news. When the dust settled, only one defendant remained, Citizens Bank. The jury deliberated a week before finding for Maxey, with a $2,689,767 verdict against the bank. At the time, it was the largest civil judgment in Lubbock's history.

The bank was hurt and vowed to appeal. Eventually, the case reached the Texas Supreme Court, which ordered a new trial. The second trial, in 1976, resulted in an even larger jury verdict against the bank: $7.5 million including interest, another record. The bank appealed; again, the case was remanded for a new trial.

By 1980, no one was looking forward to a third trial. Maxey settled with the bank for $2.2 million. He was almost seventy. Maxey and Melba bought a comfortable townhome, and he dabbled in real estate and construction until his death in 1990 at age seventy-nine. Melba died in 1995. Their daughter Glenna Goodacre became a renowned artist.

The bank slowly went downhill and eventually merged with a larger bank. Citizens Tower was abandoned and sat vacant for many years (but saw new life as Lubbock's City Hall in 2020).

Through almost fifteen years of litigation, Maxey's lawsuit against the bank involved some of the best-known legal talent from Lubbock and across Texas and produced a landmark Texas Supreme Court decision involving bank law.

# THE RICHEST MEN IN THE WORLD ONCE FACED TRIAL IN LUBBOCK

The Hunt family, longtime owners of the Kansas City Chiefs, gathered on February 2, 2020, in Miami to watch their team win the Super Bowl. Some forty-five years earlier, the same Hunt family had gathered in Lubbock for an entirely different event: a tense, high-profile criminal trial that jeopardized the freedom of two of the richest men in the world.

Bunker and Herbert Hunt were sons of legendary Texas oil billionaire H.L. Hunt, considered the world's wealthiest man in the 1970s. The brothers ran into trouble in 1969–70 when they hired private detectives to illegally wiretap the telephones of executives of their father's company, HLH Food Products Division of Hunt Oil.

Herbert (*left*) and Bunker Hunt, two of the wealthiest men ever tried for a crime in the United States, were acquitted of wiretapping by a Lubbock jury in 1975. *Public domain.*

The wiretaps, part of an internal investigation of embezzlement within HLH, were inadvertently discovered by local police, and the evidence was turned over to federal authorities.

There were reports that the Hunts attempted to thwart the Federal Bureau of Investigation's wiretapping investigation by bribing witnesses, and a clandestine meeting with President Richard Nixon at Treasury Secretary John Connally's Floresville ranch failed to halt the probe.

A Dallas grand jury indicted the Hunt brothers for obstruction of justice and interception of electronic communications, both serious federal crimes. If convicted, the Hunts each faced a maximum penalty of ten years in federal prison.

The scandal generated a tremendous amount of publicity in Dallas, so the wiretap case was transferred to Judge Halbert O. Woodward's court in Lubbock for trial. Judge Woodward was known as a fair and impartial jurist with a congenial judicial temperament. The obstruction case was postponed for a later trial.

As counsel, the Hunts wisely chose fifty-four-year-old Lubbock lawyer Travis Shelton and Virginia wiretap law expert Philip Hirschkop, thirty-nine. The lawyers were a study in contrast.

Hirschkop, described by the *Lubbock Avalanche-Journal* as "brash and arrogant," had successfully argued the 1967 U.S. Supreme Court case that ended state bans on interracial marriage. The liberal American Civil Liberties Union lawyer "seemed out of place" in West Texas, according to the *A-J*, appearing in court in battered motorcycle boots to defend members of one of the most conservative families in America. Nevertheless, Hirschkop displayed a dry sense of humor and was effective in the courtroom.

The more moderate Shelton was a native of Tahoka and had previously served as Lubbock County district attorney. A World War II veteran and Presbyterian deacon, he was known as a formidable trial attorney, described by the press as "one of the three best criminal defense lawyers in Texas, with good old-fashioned horse sense."

In addition, the Hunts retained an aggressive Denver public relations firm to provide the media with background material from their side of the story. The Hunts wanted the public to know the charges were a vendetta against the family because of its refusal to go along with the Central Intelligence Agency in supplying information on Egyptian terrorist groups and oil dealings.

Jury selection kicked off in mid-September 1975, and proceedings lasted about two weeks.

Each member of the nine-man, three-woman jury was identified by name, hometown and occupation by the *A-J*, but the panel was not sequestered. Judge Woodward threatened—but did not issue—a "gag order" to quiet trial participants, and the Hunt brothers gleefully granted many interviews during the trial.

As the jurors stood to swear their oaths before Judge Woodward, a standing-room-only crowd filled the gallery, eagerly anticipating opening statements.

The government team was led by forty-seven-year-old Frank McCown, a former district attorney from the small Panhandle town of Dalhart, appointed by Richard Nixon in 1972 as United States attorney for the Northern District of Texas. Described as "crusty and blunt," he was known as the prosecutor who ended the political careers of several powerful Texans in the Sharpstown stock-fraud scandal, including a couple of Lubbock politicians.

McCown told the jury, "A good reason, a good motive, a good purpose, is not a defense to a crime," and he repeated this theme throughout the trial.

Shelton countered, "Under certain circumstances—to protect your property—there may be a justification, a motive for wiretapping. In order to convict, the government must show an evil intent to wiretap. The defense will show the only reason for an investigation which included wiretapping was to stop a scheme by three trusted employees of the Hunt companies who were attempting to bankrupt HLH Products and Hunt Oil."

McCown summoned the private detectives who had installed the wiretaps to the witness stand. Their credibility was called into question, as the detectives had already been convicted for their part in the wiretapping scheme.

But none of the Hunt executives whose phones were tapped were called as witnesses. The prosecutor's reluctance to call the witnesses was understandable, as the "victims" of the wiretapping had been imprisoned for embezzling from the Hunt companies.

The forty-ish brothers admitted they had ordered the phone taps but said they were unaware—and their private detectives never told them—that wiretapping employees was illegal.

Despite their immense wealth, Bunker and Herbert Hunt cultivated an image as unpretentious good ol' boys. They drove old Cadillacs, flew coach and stayed at a modest hotel when they showed up in Lubbock for their 1975 wiretapping trial. Bunker was said to be "the kind of guy who orders chicken-fried steak and Jell-O, spills some on his tie, and then goes out and buys all the silver in the world."

Clad in inexpensive suits, the brothers testified in their own defense. Bunker, described as "bespectacled and chubby," spoke in a soft-spoken mumble. He said the reason for wiretaps was to expose embezzlement within the Hunt companies. "I thought it was perfectly legal. I would not do anything illegal."

Herbert, distinguished-looking with graying black hair, testified on the verge of tears, telling an attentive jury he and his brother "could not stand by and let that happen to Dad."

A parade of employees and members of the Hunt family testified the embezzlement within the Hunt empire totaled nearly $50 million. If the theft had continued, Hunt Oil would have been bankrupted, they said.

A second parade of notable witnesses followed to attest to the good character of the Hunt brothers, including Houston Oilers owner Bud Adams and former Texas Tech football star E.J. Holub.

Prosecutor Frank McCown argued for conviction, saying the Hunt brothers had acted with evil motive and evil intent. "All the Hunts wanted was money," he said, but conceded, "I doubt that there will ever be a jury that will have to stand in so much awe of people."

In response, Lubbock criminal defense lawyer Travis Shelton observed, "There is something odd about this case." In his twenty-seven years of practice, he had never seen a trial in which no complaining witness was called by the prosecution.

Shelton challenged the jury, "If you can find a bad purpose or an evil intent in what they did, then you can convict them!" News accounts described Shelton's rousing final argument as "almost evangelistic oratory."

As many as twenty members of the Hunt family were present during portions of the trial, seen as a show of family unity at a time the Hunts were said to be involved in a huge family feud over patriarch H.L.'s fortune. The billionaire had died the previous year.

On September 26, some forty members of the Hunt family packed Lubbock's modest, windowless federal district courtroom in anticipation of the verdict. The combined wealth of those in attendance may have reached $3 billion ($15 billion in current dollars). Among the spectators was the defendant's younger brother Lamar Hunt, owner of the Kansas City Chiefs, accompanied by his wife, Norma Hunt.

Gasps of relief filled the chamber when Judge Halbert O. Woodward read the jury's "not guilty" verdict. A grin wrinkled the face of the portly Bunker. A more subdued Herbert showed little emotion.

"My heart goes out to ordinary people, and poor people who can't afford proper defense," said Bunker. "If we'd just been ordinary folks, I'm afraid we would have been in trouble." Indeed, the Hunt brothers were among the wealthiest individuals ever tried for a crime.

Their attorneys later negotiated a dismissal of the second indictment alleging obstruction, but it was not the end of the Hunt brothers' legal troubles. Well before the Lubbock trial, Bunker, Herbert and Lamar had attempted to corner the global silver market. When silver prices collapsed in 1980, they lost $1 billion and faced civil conspiracy charges. They paid a record multimillion-dollar judgment and declared bankruptcy, but family fortunes eventually recovered.

H.L. Hunt's fifteen children wrangled over his multibillion-dollar estate for many years, and vestiges of family lawsuits lingered almost a half century following his death.

Today, Herbert is in his nineties and lives in Dallas. He has an estimated net worth exceeding $3 billion. Bunker spent much of his remaining years breeding Thoroughbred racehorses and died in 2014. Lamar—founder of the American Football League—died in 2006, leaving the Kansas City Chiefs to his four children and his widow, Norma. The descendants of H.L. are collectively worth an estimated $15 billion.

Some observers said the Hunt case was Judge Woodward's most important, but history tells a different story. Woodward (1918–2000) presided over *United States v. Lubbock Independent School District* between 1970 and 1992, which resulted in desegregation of Lubbock public schools.

Travis Shelton (1921–2003) went on to be elected president of the State Bar of Texas and was inducted into the Texas Criminal Defense Lawyers Hall of Fame. His fee for successfully representing the richest family in the world is unknown, but the Hunt brothers complained their legal fees were "very high." The *New York Times* reported the Hunts paid their attorneys almost $1 million (worth $4 million today), arguably a pittance for billionaires. But whatever Shelton's share of the Hunt fortune, it was certainly well earned— decent wages for a Lubbock lawyer.

## THE DIRTY MOVIE WARS: LAST TANGO IN LUBBOCK

During the 1970s, police raided local theaters regularly, confiscated "dirty movies" and arrested owners and managers for displaying obscenity. The raids were front-page news and led to high-profile criminal trials. Lubbock was the setting for the first obscenity jury trial in the United States involving the celebrated movie *Last Tango in Paris*.

The 1972 French film, starring Marlon Brando and directed by Bernardo Bertolucci, portrays a recently widowed American who begins an anonymous sexual relationship with a young Parisian woman. *Tango* generated intense international controversy because of its unusual plot and raw portrayal of sexual violence. Brando and Bertolucci were both nominated for Oscars, and the movie generated big revenues in the United States.

*Tango* was screened at Lubbock's Fox Twin Theater in August 1973. Soon, Lubbock County criminal district attorney Alton Griffin asked Lubbock police detective Butch Hargrave to investigate. Hargrave drafted a search and seizure warrant application before viewing the movie, then took a magistrate and a prosecutor to the Fox. After the three watched a portion of the film, the magistrate signed the warrant, and *Tango* was seized. Fox customers' ticket money was refunded as another five hundred patrons waiting for the next show were turned away. Fox manager Ralph Boyd was later arrested and charged with the misdemeanor offense of "exhibiting an obscene movie."

*Last Tango in Paris* starred Marlon Brando and Maria Schneider. *Public domain.*

The case was tried in Judge Denzil Bevers's County Court at Law No. 2. Lawyers and jurors were faced with a new Texas law. "A film must meet three conditions before it can be ruled obscene: Appeals to a prurient interest in sex, nudity or excretion; is patently offensive because it affronts contemporary standards relating to the description of or reproduction of sex, nudity or excretion; and is utterly without redeeming social value."

The trial began on November 13, 1973. After five women and one man were chosen as jurors, prosecutor Griffin called his only witness, Detective Hargrave. Hargrave recounted his actions at the theater, and the movie was introduced as evidence. Judge Bevers temporarily relocated the trial to the Fox, a popular theater offering first-run movies. About one hundred trial participants, media representatives and trial spectators viewed the entire film.

Back at the courthouse, Griffin rested his case, and defense attorneys Dan Hurley and Mike Worley began calling numerous witnesses who testified that the movie did not appeal to their "prurient interest" but did offer "redeeming social value." Griffin aggressively challenged the opinions of professors, housewives, professionals and common citizens, and contentious litigation stretched over two days.

During final arguments, Griffin told the jury, "If people watch 'Last Tango in Paris,' they will be influenced to engage in the same sorts of activities depicted in the film." Hurley responded sarcastically: "Mr. Griffin is right. I remember when I watched 'Cinderella,' I started wearing a tutu and glass slippers and danced all through the house!" The defense accused Griffin of "trying to tell people what they can hear and ultimately what they can think."

The jury deliberated two hours before returning a "not guilty" verdict. Theater manager Boyd was acquitted. Hurley told the press, "It was a wonderful victory for the people of Lubbock. Movies with social value are not obscene."

Griffin was unapologetic. "I don't write the law. If people don't like the laws, they should contact their legislator, not me." He said he called only one witness because, "It would have been an insult to the intelligence of the jury. The movie was the best evidence."

*Tango* reappeared without incident at the venerable Lindsay Theater in downtown Lubbock in February 1975.

Authorities continued raiding movie houses, seizing films such as the infamous *Deep Throat, Prostitution Pornography U.S.A.* and a picture known only as *Nick*.... Some defendants were convicted, others were acquitted. Young Lubbock lawyer John Montford handled several obscenity cases for the defense.

Controversy arose on April 4, 1975, when the *Lubbock Avalanche-Journal* published a prominent article titled "'Deep Throat,' Other Porno Films Available to 'Select Few.'" Police property sheets indicated that as many as fifty law-enforcement officials had signed out seized pornographic films from the property vault. Assistant CDA Tom Sawyer kept *Deep Throat* for a week, explaining to the *A-J*, "I got it to show to a group of Tech students in my office who were studying pornography."

Assistant CDA Wayne Reaud, who borrowed multiple seized films, told the *A-J* that he had intended to show them to a defense lawyer representing a theater owner, but the lawyer decided not to view the films.

The movie *Nick...* was especially popular with the Lubbock Police Department. Detective Hargrave checked it out of the property room twice, Corporal Teddy Daniel three times and Captain Wayne Love once.

Movie seizures dwindled, and in 1978, Griffin was defeated as CDA by Montford, who had successfully defended a theater owner in the *Prostitution Pornography U.S.A.* trial.

# 5

# LAWYERS AND THEIR HAUNTS

## Temple Houston:
## Prairie Dog Lawyer of the Plains

He was said to be the best shot in the West. "Old Betsy," his white-handled Colt revolver, was always strapped to his waist. He wore beautifully tailored buckskin attire from Mexico and a handwoven sombrero with an exceedingly wide brim, a silver eagle displayed against its high crown.

Like his father, he stood more than six feet tall. His auburn hair was shoulder-length, and his eyes were steely gray. His knowledge of the Bible and classical literature was encyclopedic.

When he spoke, everyone listened. The man was not an outlaw or a gunslinger, nor a preacher. No one dared call him a dandy.

He was Temple Lea Houston, the most celebrated and colorful of the prairie dog lawyers, pioneer advocates who chased justice on the Texas and Oklahoma plains in the late nineteenth century.

Born in the Texas Governor's Mansion in 1860, Temple was the youngest son of Sam Houston, iconic soldier, first president of the Republic of Texas, U.S. senator and governor of Tennessee and the Lone Star State.

Temple left home at age thirteen to join a cattle drive and later worked on a riverboat on the Mississippi River. After a stint as a U.S. Senate page, he graduated with honors from Baylor University, majoring in law and philosophy. At age twenty-one, he became the youngest licensed lawyer in Texas.

Two years later, Temple was appointed the first district attorney for the Texas Panhandle, based in Mobeetie, Wheeler County. His district covered fourteen thousand square miles—about the size of Switzerland—but had few residents and only two other towns, Tascosa and Clarendon.

He prosecuted murder, assault, stock theft and prostitution cases. Gambling was also illegal, but Temple said, "It would have been impossible to enforce Texas's gaming statutes without arresting the entire populace."

He developed a reputation as a fierce advocate and a magnificent orator. During sessions of court, people came from throughout the area to witness the courtroom drama, camping out for several days. It was worth the loss of time from farming or ranching to watch "Old Sam's boy" perform.

Temple Houston about the time he was appointed district attorney. *Courtesy Texas State Library and Archives.*

He was elected state senator in 1884, the youngest in Texas history at age twenty-four.

In 1888, a crowd of fifty thousand heard Temple's speech dedicating the new Texas Capitol building at Austin.

By the 1890s, Temple was a criminal defense attorney. Accounts of his courtroom performances are legendary. In 1899, he defended Minnie Stacey, a "soiled dove" of the Oklahoma Territory. His impromptu "Plea for a Fallen Woman" in summation is regarded as a legal classic:

> *You heard with what cold cruelty the prosecution referred to the sins of this woman, as if her condition were of her own preference. The evidence has painted you a picture of her life and surroundings. Do you think that they were embraced of her own choosing? Do you think that she willingly embraced a life so revolting and horrible? Ah, no! Gentlemen....Our sex wrecked her once pure life...and only in the friendly shelter of the grave can her betrayed and broken heart ever find the Redeemer's promised rest.*
>
> *If the prosecutors of the woman whom you are trying had brought her before the Savior, they would have accepted His challenge and each one gathered a rock and stoned her, in the twinkling of an eye. No, Gentlemen, do as your Master did twice under the same circumstances that surround you. Tell her to go in peace.*

The all-male jury quickly acquitted Minnie Stacey.

Temple defended a man accused of murder. During final argument, he dramatically demonstrated the terror his client felt to be threatened by an experienced gunman.

> *What would any of you worthy gentlemen have done in the face of such a character? Do you have any idea how you would have fared against the lightening draw of a gun-artist—unless you had drawn first? This malefactor was so adept with a six-shooter that he could place a gun in the hands of an inexperienced man, then draw and fire his own weapon before his victim could pull the trigger. Like this!*

He suddenly whipped "Old Betsy" from beneath his frock coat, pointed the revolver directly at the jury and emptied it rapidly.

The jury and everyone in the courtroom scattered. When court resumed, Temple assured the court he had fired blanks. The jury quickly returned a verdict of guilty.

Temple moved for a new trial, arguing that the jurors had violated their duty to remain sequestered. The judge was obliged to follow the law and granted a new trial. Months later, Temple's client was acquitted by a different jury.

He shot two men dead in separate Oklahoma bar fights, but Temple beat both murder cases. In 1905, he died of natural causes at age forty-five.

# AS LUBBOCK GREW, SO DID ITS JAILS

When Lubbock County was organized in March 1891, Sheriff William Lay had no hoosegow to hold the hooligans he arrested, so judges were obliged to entrust defendants to their lawyers' custody to await trial. Offenders without lawyers apparently just went home, but soon there was a place to house the citizens accused.

In May, the Lubbock County Commissioner's Court approved a $3,700 bid for construction of the village's first public building, the Lubbock County Jail, a rough, boxlike, two-room frame structure. The jail was located near the northeast corner of the rectangular two-block town square, sharing space with a solitary windmill and water tank.

The lockup offered accommodation for much more than just prisoners. The jailhouse provided a temporary place to congregate for the churches of

Lubbock—Methodist, Baptist and Quaker—and served the tiny community as a social center.

Lubbock's first schoolteacher, Minnie Tubbs, taught in the jail building in the fall of 1891. Later that year, a two-story frame courthouse was constructed, enabling churches and schools to use the new county building as their meeting place, rather than the jail.

The jail was later enlarged to three rooms, but in 1909, it was destroyed by fire. In 1911, a new three-story red-brick jail featuring indoor plumbing and heating was erected on the east end of the square, at a cost of $14,000.

The second jail provided living quarters for the sheriff. Sheriff C.A. Holcomb and his family resided on the main floor for four years. The sheriff's wife cooked meals for inmates, and three of the couple's ten children were born in the jail.

At times, Lubbock County's second jail was almost empty. In April 1920, it housed just three prisoners, two of whom were being held for Crosby County crimes.

Lubbock's architecturally significant third jailhouse was completed in 1931. The jail's $148,000 price tag paid for the shell of the building, with interior work and cells to be completed later, helping create local employment during the Great Depression.

Third Lubbock County Jail. *Courtesy Southwest Collection, Special Collections Library, Texas Tech University.*

The exterior of the jail, a three-story poured-concrete facility, was of distinctive Art Deco design by local architect Sylvan B. Haynes. The building, still intact at Main Street and Buddy Holly Avenue, was listed in the National Register of Historic Places in 2018.

In 1951, two floors were added, bringing the jail to a height of five stories. A tunnel connected the jail to the new 1950 courthouse. In 1960, another five-story addition to the west brought the building to its current thirty-five thousand square feet of space.

Male inmates were housed on the third and fourth floors. Women and juveniles were housed separately on the fifth floor. The kitchen and housing for jail trustees was located on the second floor. Inmates were carefully segregated by race. Booking areas, the infirmary and offices occupied the main floor.

Jailers escorted attorneys to visit clients via a single elevator. Jail cells were in the interior of the building, with a "walkaround" hallway separating cells from exterior windows. Lawyers used the walkaround to visit clients.

One day, after a young lawyer completed his consultation with a client, he buzzed the jailer to usher him downstairs. No jailer appeared, seemingly for hours.

Finally, the lawyer yelled through an open window to pedestrians below, "Help me! I'm a lawyer, and I can't get out of here!" Without looking up, a passerby replied, "You're a lawyer? You're right where you belong!"

Multiple jail breaks plagued the 1931 facility. In January 1969, three prisoners threatened jailers with makeshift knives and fled. All were soon recaptured. Eleven inmates escaped on July 12, 1974, but only ten were recaptured. Four unsuccessful breakouts involving six prisoners happened within a six-month period in 1983.

In 1980, a large addition to the Lubbock County Jail was completed to the east of the 1931 structure. Sheriff Sonny Keesee refused to provide private visitation cells for attorneys to consult with clients in the new facility. Lawyers were obliged to share public visitation spaces with inmates' family members and other callers.

A federal lawsuit was filed against the sheriff and Lubbock County by the Lubbock Criminal Defense Lawyers Association. Settlement of the litigation resulted in the construction of private attorney-client visitation cells on the first floor of the 1931 jail.

In 2010, the state-of-the-art Lubbock County Detention Center was completed. Located six miles north of downtown Lubbock on Holly Avenue, the $100 million, half-million-square-foot space can accommodate 1,512 prisoners and is staffed by 362 employees.

The 1980 jail addition adjacent to the 1931 Lubbock County Jail was recently renovated for the Sheriff's Department Law Enforcement Center at a cost of about $7.7 million.

The deteriorating 1931 jail continued to house overflow prisoners and provide office space well into the 2000s. It was placed on Preservation Texas's "Most Endangered List" in 2016 and sold for $200,000 in 2017. The new owners, Tulsa businessmen John Snyder and Jim Snyder, are in the process of transforming the old jail for use as apartments.

# THE FIRST LUBBOCK COUNTY COURTHOUSE

Lubbock County's first courthouse was literally—and figuratively—the center of the community. By today's standards, it was little more than a two-story wood shack, but the building served the people's needs for many years.

Early in 1891, Lubbock County organizers established the seat of local government, near its geographic center, on a two-block rectangular tract of land purchased from a "Mr. Farris," for $1,920. Soon, the Dallas architectural firm Gill, Woodward & Gill designed a modest courthouse.

The structure was to be forty-eight feet wide, fifty-six feet long and twenty-four feet high, at a proposed cost of $12,000. Court minutes indicate that lumber for the project could be purchased at "Amorillo" or Colorado City, the nearest railheads.

During construction, the Lubbock County Commissioner's Court met in what was identified in court minutes as a "house used as a courthouse." Later, commissioners met in a building on the northwest corner of Texas Avenue and Broadway owned by W.M. Lay, Lubbock County's first sheriff. The commissioners then moved to W.E. Rayner's building, which was rented until the courthouse was completed.

By the close of 1891, county government was being conducted in a proud and imposing whitewashed wood structure, the largest public building within hundreds of miles. The style was Italianate, featuring a peaked roof and a distinctive square tower terminating in a steeple, known architecturally as a cupola.

The cupola did not last long. In 1895, a huge windstorm hit the town. The courthouse was so twisted that doors would not shut, and the central tower was blown away. The roof had to be removed before the building could be squared. In the rebuilding, the cupola was not replaced.

The 1891 Lubbock County Courthouse. *Courtesy Southwest Collection, Special Collections Library, Texas Tech University.*

The courthouse square, surrounded by a scattered business district, was the focal point of all activity in the little village, populated by fewer than three hundred souls at the time. A windmill on the square provided a communal trough. For many years, the trough was the town's only civic water supply.

Public barbecue pits were dug on the east side of the square. Locust trees provided by Lubbock County clerk George Wolffarth from his farm north of town (now Lubbock Country Club)—interspersed with hitching posts and tie rails—surrounded the seat of government.

Original Lubbock County Courthouse, circa 1900, years after the loss of the cupola in a violent sandstorm. *Courtesy Cindy Martin.*

With its shady lawn, the courthouse square was a favorite gathering spot. On Sunday afternoons, families often brought picnic baskets to long tables on the courthouse lawn and, after a leisurely lunch, spent the afternoon visiting with friends.

A bandstand was built on the square, and in addition to playing for dances, parties and special events, the Lubbock Band (organized in 1891) gave concerts and benefit performances until the early 1920s.

Dances were held at the courthouse, a "Literary Society" was organized and met there and an organ was installed in one of the second-floor rooms for church services and community singing.

Alas, in 1906, county fathers ruled that the courthouse could no longer host dances.

In the early years, church congregations held services at the courthouse. The Church of Christ, Quakers, Baptists and Methodists each worshipped at the courthouse on successive Sundays. Many people attended services each week at the courthouse, regardless of the auspices under which they were held.

Two interesting criminal cases were tried in the original courthouse. In 1892, Jim Vance—described as "a boy"—was accused of horse theft. He was acquitted in Lubbock County's first jury trial. In 1912, Lubbock city marshal William Taylor was acquitted of murder in the shooting deaths of two men at the Blue Front Restaurant.

Early photos of the courthouse depict "Uncle Tang" Martin. According to legend, Uncle Tang fought in the Civil War and later captained a packet boat on the Mississippi River. He ended his career as a cowboy on the South Plains.

As an old man, Uncle Tang lost his legs due to an infection. County commissioners provided him a wheelchair, living space in the courthouse, and a ramp for access. He became the unofficial greeter to courthouse visitors, spawning many interesting stories.

One night, he snuck into a store looking for liquid refreshment. By mistake, he fumbled for a bottle of bluing solution, spilling the laundry product on his long white beard. The next day, with his blue beard, he had a hard time successfully defending his innocence. When Uncle Tang died, the town turned out for a large funeral.

The next step in courthouse growth came in 1915, when $100,000 was authorized for a new Lubbock County Courthouse.

To make way for the new courthouse, the 1891 structure was moved to the southwest corner of Tenth Street and Avenue G so that county business could be conducted without interruption during construction.

After it was moved, there is no record of what became of the original courthouse, site of so much of Lubbock's early history. The current Lubbock County Courthouse was completed in 1950.

## Daniel Boone's Relative: First Female Lubbock Lawyer

In 1910, only three women were licensed Texas attorneys. By 1930, a whopping 75 female lawyers practiced in the state, along with about 6,500 male colleagues. Today, women make up about 35 percent of 90,000 Texas lawyers. One early female lawyer was the first of her gender to practice law in Lubbock.

Born in 1888, Emma K. Boone was a native of Hill County, Texas, and a descendant of Squire Boone, brother of the iconic Kentucky frontiersman Daniel Boone. She attended Southwest Texas State Normal School (now Texas State University) and Baylor University.

In 1916, Emma enrolled at the University of Texas School of Law, joining only six female students there. She was the first female president of the UT junior law class. While in law school, she married William H. Bledsoe of Lubbock, in 1917. (Emma was Bledsoe's second wife. His first wife, Alice Matthews, died in 1915.) Bledsoe at the time served as state representative from the South Plains area, so they probably met in Austin.

After Emma received her law degree, Judge Whitfield Davidson administered an oath that made her the first woman admitted to the bar in Lubbock County. It was 1918, but another two years would pass before the United States Constitution was amended to allow Emma and all American women the right to vote, on August 18, 1920.

W.H. Bledsoe was a legendary, self-educated pioneer Lubbock lawyer who began his practice in 1908. He successfully defended the first person tried for murder in Lubbock County, in 1912. As state senator, he brought Texas Technological College to Lubbock by sponsoring the 1923 enabling legislation. Emma said in a 1969 interview: "Mr. Chitwood put the bill through the House. It was known as the Bledsoe-Chitwood bill, but I know who wrote it because the Judge [Bledsoe] and I went over every sentence." Senator Bledsoe was a founder of the law firm now known as Crenshaw, Dupree & Milam.

Emma K., as she preferred to be called, maintained a civil practice for a time. In the 1920s, her husband asked her to speak for his client in a murder trial. It was well before Texas women were permitted to serve on juries (1954). An experienced old judge advised her that the all-male jury would certainly be offended if she spoke, so Emma K. declined for the benefit of the client.

She was an educator for many years, first in high schools and then at Texas Tech, where she taught Texas history. Her granddaughter, Bronwen Bledsoe of New York, remembers Emma as a well-dressed, well-traveled socialite who practiced little law.

Senator Bledsoe died in 1936, and Emma remained in their handsome brick home at 1812 Broadway until her death at age ninety-five in 1983. Lubbock attorney Pat Simek acquired the Bledsoe home and converted it to a law office in the mid-1980s. He continues to maintain his practice in the historic building, which was constructed in 1921. At the time of her death, Emma was survived by a son, seven grandchildren, fourteen great-grandchildren and fifteen great-great-grandchildren.

Emma paved the way for the amazing success of the second woman who practiced law in Lubbock, Pat S. Moore, a native of Lorenzo. Moore began her practice in Lubbock in 1949 after graduating from SMU Law School. In 1953, she became the first female president of the Lubbock County Bar Association, and four years later, she became the first woman elected to Lubbock County public office, as judge of Lubbock County Court at Law Number 2.

Emma K. Bledsoe (*right*) with Peggy Shurtleff and Pueblo Indians, 1914. *Author's collection.*

In 1968, she was elected Lubbock County's first female district judge, of the 72nd District Court. She presided over many notable cases, including the first *Maxey v. Citizens National Bank* trial, the longest civil litigation in Lubbock's history.

She was instrumental in establishing Texas Boys Ranch, where troubled juvenile males of Lubbock and surrounding counties could live rather than return from her courtroom to their unsafe, unsupervised, unlawful homes. Texas Boys Ranch is now a part of Children's Home of Lubbock.

Judge Moore received statewide publicity when she refused to seek an excuse from jury duty, stepping down from her own bench to report for jury duty in the 99th District Court. She was not chosen but was paid for two days' service, then endorsed the check back to Lubbock County.

Judge Moore's accomplishments came despite a severe disability caused by a childhood bout with polio, and she died tragically of cancer at age forty-nine. She was survived by her husband, James, also a Lubbock attorney, and two children.

The Junior League of Lubbock created the Pat S. Moore Award in 1974 in her honor. The award recognizes women who, despite adverse circumstances, provide outstanding inspiration to others and service to the community and who possess the preeminent qualities of integrity, morality, loyalty, humility, compassion and courage.

# 6

# EVOLUTION OF CULTURE ON THE TEXAS PLAINS

## HISTORIC NEWSPAPERS AND NEWSMEN
## OF THE SOUTH PLAINS

When Old Lubbock and Monterey merged to form the village of Lubbock in early 1891, there was no local newspaper to chronicle the historic event. Soon, young lawyer Robert E. Lee Rogers left the fading community of Estacado and scrambled to establish a weekly newspaper, the *Lubbock Leader*.

Rogers probably knew the value of a good local periodical, as Estacado was the home of the original South Plains newspaper, the *Crosby County News*, first published in November 1886. John Watts Murray, a forty-four-year-old Confederate Civil War veteran, moved a small printing plant from Foard County to establish the venture.

In a county of less than eight hundred souls, the *Crosby County News* was dependent on advertising support from Colorado City and Amarillo, towns more than one hundred miles away. The *News* became the pioneer booster of the plains. Several hundred copies of the *News* were mailed each week to all parts of the country. Cattlemen objected to the newspaper's glowing promotion of agricultural opportunity, hoping to slow South Plains settlement and the end of the range. The *News* moved to the new county seat at Emma in about 1891.

Another newspaper that pre-dated the *Lubbock Leader* was the *Hale County Herald*, established in October 1889. Its slogan was, "Nothing Shallow but the Water."

The first issue of the *Lubbock Leader* hit town on July 31, 1891. In a proud statement, Rogers wrote, "Lubbock, the county seat of Lubbock County, is only about four months old and now has 250 people, making Lubbock here to stay." The first newspaper was published in a building on Avenue G, between Main and Broadway, near the present Lubbock County Sheriff's Office.

The major news was of opportunity. "There is in this county 190,324 acres of school land ready for actual settlers. This land can be bought for $2 per acre and…forty years to pay it, at 5 per cent interest.

"There is also in Lubbock County 10,000 acres of vacant Public Domain, subject to homestead. A married man can take up to 100 acres of this land and obtain a title to it by living on it 3 years. Entire cost will not exceed $21—an unmarried man may take up 80 acres under the same rule."

The two-page newspaper featured advertising for seemingly all of the little hamlet's merchants: Singer's store, Caldwell's store, the Nicolett Hotel, Sanders and Wolffarth's Livery Stable, Moore and Wheelock's Livery Stable, Sanders and Lewis' Liquor Emporium, Hunt and Jones Land Office. A barbershop operated by Ed T. Cox advertised, as did W.P. Phenix's blacksmith shop and a laundry run by G.W. Lee.

Professionals also posted ads in the first *Leader*. Two local attorneys, W.F. Hendrix and W.C. Henderson, promoted their law practices as well as assistance in insurance and real estate matters. A physician, C.G. Austin, MD, announced plans to open a general practice in Lubbock and the surrounding area. An itemization of "Lubbock wants" from the first edition of the *Leader* included a drugstore, a shoe shop and a tack shop.

Another early newspaper, the *Texan Press*, established in Estacado on August 30, 1890, consolidated with the *Lubbock Leader* in October 1892. The paper, now known as the *Texan Press-Leader*, was edited and published by M.M. Cox.

James Winford Hunt—later founder and president of McMurry College—soon became editor of the *Press-Leader*, published in Lubbock until 1899. The twenty-five-year-old Hunt then moved his print operation to Plainview and restored the newspaper's original name, the *Texan Press*, which eventually evolved into the *Plainview News*.

Lubbock was without a newspaper for about a year when, on May 4, 1900, thirty-one-year-old J.J. Dillard and twenty-seven-year-old Thad Tubbs began publication of the weekly *Lubbock Avalanche*.

Tubbs—described as a "professional gambler"—hooked two horses to a wagon and rode to Amarillo, the nearest railhead. He loaded a press, a case of type and paper stock the entrepreneurs ordered from Connecticut for $175.

Traveling home through Hale Center, someone asked, "What you got there, Thad?" He answered, "Oh, I'm starting a newspaper." The man threw a silver dollar in the wagon and said, "Send it to me!" Thus, the unidentified Hale Center resident became the first subscriber of the *Avalanche*.

Dillard, a lawyer who later became Lubbock County judge, explained the reason for the publication's name. He said the press was secretly unloaded at night. "We wanted to bring the printing equipment in and circulate a paper before any information leaked out and do it suddenly—like an avalanche hits."

J.J. Dillard, first editor of the *Lubbock Avalanche*, circa 1900. *Courtesy Southwest Collection, Special Collections Library, Texas Tech University.*

Priced at a nickel each, the first edition of forty copies sold out quickly. The fourteen-by-eleven-inch-format paper was four pages with four columns of news. Printed in the back room of a one-story frame building on the northeast corner of Main and Texas, the paper shared space with Dillard's law office in the front room.

The *Avalanche* was an immediate success, despite less than three hundred Lubbock County residents as prospective subscribers. "There was nothing but abject prairie, with one or two business houses on the north side of the square, about the same number west," editor J.J. Dillard remembered. Nevertheless, the paper's slogan reflected optimism for the community: "The Hub of the Plains."

The *Avalanche* also published a "Lubbock Wants" list: "An implement firm; a furniture store; a photograph gallery; a lumber yard; a jeweler and repair shop; a national bank; a telephone line to Canyon City by way of Plainview; all the honest upright people who desire to make their home where they will be surrounded with good moral influences and where there are no saloons and gambling dens to allure their children to vice."

Owners Dillard and Tubbs bought the press of the *Dickens Doings* in 1901 and moved it to Lubbock. The press was hand-turned and printed two pages simultaneously. In about 1903, a cylinder press, a paper cutter, cabinets and new type were purchased. "And we got a gas engine—the second gas power plant in Texas west of Fort Worth. Amarillo had the other," Dillard recalled.

Dillard bought out Tubbs' interest in the *Avalanche* in 1902, and in 1908, James L. Dow purchased the paper. Dow, age thirty, had been in the newspaper business in Colorado City, Sweetwater and Gail before he moved to Lubbock.

By 1912, eighteen hundred subscribers—half the population of Lubbock County—received the newspaper. The *Avalanche* increased in size and in volume of business until additional help was needed. Soon, new equipment was purchased and the paper, still hand-set, employed some fifteen to twenty workers and printed from sixteen to twenty-four pages each week.

The *Avalanche* office was destroyed by fire in 1913. Equipment was replaced, but many important files of the paper were lost. In 1918, a linotype machine was installed, greatly facilitating the publishing ability of the now semiweekly paper. The *Avalanche* became the first daily newspaper on the South Plains in 1922. A new weekly, the *Plains Journal*, appeared in 1924,

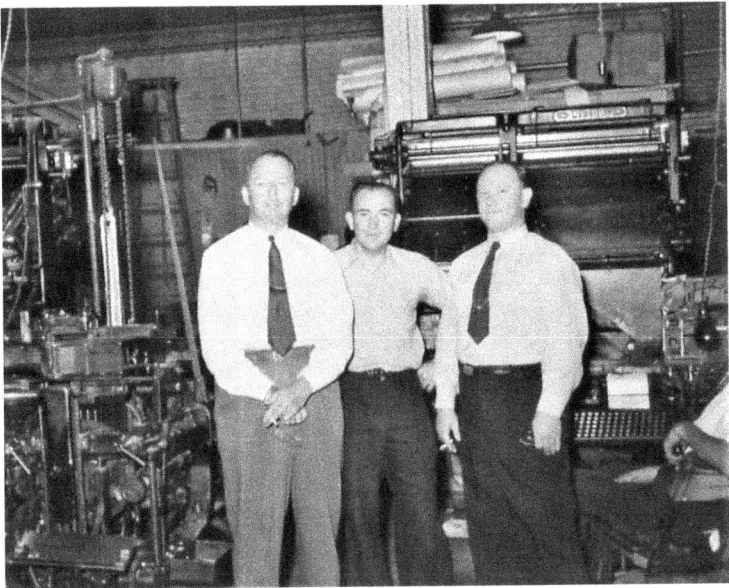

Longtime editor Charles Guy (*left*) poses with *Lubbock Avalanche-Journal* employees, 1945. *Courtesy Southwest Collection, Special Collections Library, Texas Tech University.*

with twenty-four-year-old Charles A. Guy as editor and publisher. Guy soon started a daily afternoon publication, the *Lubbock Daily Journal.*

In September 1926, Guy and a partner acquired the *Avalanche* and consolidated operations, publishing daily under three names, the *Lubbock Morning Avalanche*, the *Lubbock Evening Journal* and the Sunday *Lubbock Avalanche-Journal*, with Guy as editor. The new enterprise was officially announced in the paper. "The consolidation of the two companies here opens a new era in South Plains newspaper history and the combined organizations will be able to better serve their city and territory." The paper subscribed to modern wire services, the Associated Press and United Press International.

Originally published at what is now 1211 Texas Avenue, where the Mahon Federal Building stands, the *A-J* was relocated to the current newspaper building at 710 Avenue J in 1959. The building contained 82,000 square feet on 3.67 acres of downtown property. Over the years, the newspaper plant was increased to 137,000 square feet.

By 1959, circulation exceeded sixty-six thousand, with more than 250 regular *A-J* employees and numerous others involved in preparation and distribution of the publication. Guy remained as editor and publisher until 1972. For forty-five years, he authored a popular regular column, The Plainsman.

On his retirement, Guy wrote:

> *It has been my good fortune to write from cow camps, to the jingling of spurs in the pre-dawn hour as a roundup opened another day of branding; from the gaunt, red stone Capitol in Austin, and from the smoke-filled hotel rooms where politicians haggled. One column was written in the ornate office suite of the Speaker of the House in Washington; from personal visits in the big Oval Office with three Presidents; from the sub-basement fortress in the Pentagon and from two other places where the red "button" rests.*

As mass communications hub of the South Plains, the *A-J* chronicled countless major news stories—the rise of agriculture, the arrival of railroads, the establishment of Texas Technological College, the 1970 Lubbock tornado—while providing valuable commercial ad space and vivid accounts of local and area society, business, sports and entertainment.

With the advance of modern digital communications, television news and social networking platforms, the U.S. newspaper industry has declined, resulting in closures, mergers and circulation decreases.

The *A-J*'s evening edition ceased publication in the 1980s. In 1997, the *A-J* added digital content with LubbockOnline.com. It launched a full-color lifestyle publication, *Lubbock Magazine*, in April 2008. In February 2011, the *A-J* became the first media company on the South Plains to launch an application for iPad.

The *A-J* ran through a string of owners over the years and is now published by Gannett Company of Virginia. Circulation is approximately thirty-two thousand Monday through Friday and forty-one thousand on Sundays.

## HISTORIC LUBBOCK MOVIE THEATERS

Lubbock movie history began not with a bang, but with a silent black-and-white anonymous whimper, in a wood frame building at the northeast corner of Broadway and Avenue J. This was Lubbock's first two-story commercial structure, housing the Richardson and Tubbs furniture store on the ground floor.

The second floor was known as the Band Hall, accessible by an outdoor open staircase. Inside, there were dressing rooms, a stage and seating for about 300 patrons. Illuminated by kerosene lamps, the setting was described as "the nicest hall on the South Plains." Opened in about 1905, the Band Hall was the little town's first dedicated cultural center, replacing the courthouse as the main venue for plays, concerts, dances, and even itinerant church services.

On August 5, 1907, the *Lubbock Avalanche* reported that a nameless "moving picture show" was exhibited at the Band Hall. A second unknown movie was screened three days later. Perhaps the fifteen-minute blockbuster *Ben Hur* was shown, or the first ninety-minute feature-length film, *The Prodigal Son*, both produced in 1907. No one knows, but it is certain that the Band Hall movies were black-and-white and silent, and there is no evidence of film entertainment in Lubbock for another two years.

With the arrival of the railroad in 1909, the Hub City became a boomtown and needed a larger, more modern venue for cultural activity. The Band Hall faded, and in early 1909, the Opera House opened at the corner of Thirteenth and Avenue J, a site later occupied by Hemphill-Wells Department Store. The rickety one-story frame building, about thirty by ninety feet, offered a large variety of "high class entertainment of different kinds" as well as "a very elaborate and up-to-date selection" of silent movies, according to the *Avalanche*.

Elaborate drop curtains were decorated with glamorous advertisements by local merchants. The building was heated by coal stoves, one in the front and one in the rear, and "noisy lamps overhead hindered perfect hearing for the appreciative audience," a patron recalled. The movie projection booth was originally at the front of the building, where it obstructed the view and presented a fire hazard. Lubbock was still a town without electricity, so a gasoline generator was employed to power the projector and fifty to sixty lights. Since no customer would be satisfied without proper refreshments, the "Opera Confectionery" offered treats next door.

The Opera House was managed by Bill Payne, a former barber. He advertised his attractions by riding his horse through the streets of Lubbock, shouting into a megaphone, "Five hundred feet of movie film at the Opera House tonight! Hurry, hurry, show starts right away!" Wearing his pants tucked into shiny boots, with a long coat, large red bow tie and tall silk hat, he invariably attracted the desired attention.

The Opera House hosted the first commencement exercises of Lubbock High School in May 1909. A month later, Presbyterian church services were held at the Opera House.

The *Avalanche* reported the opening of a new venture in April 1909, the Orpheum, built by Lubbock entrepreneurs Charles Reppert and Jinks Penny. The newspaper reported that the Orpheum screened "movies every night." It is unclear whether the Orpheum and the Opera House were separate theaters. The businesses may have merged, as the Opera House became known as the Orpheum Opera House within a matter of weeks. A map found in the Southwest Collection of Texas Tech University indicates that the Orpheum Opera House was in the 1200 block of Texas Avenue in July 1909. Business eventually slowed, and the theater closed in 1911.

Enter Erving McElroy, a trained stonecutter who worked as a cowboy before arriving in Lubbock in 1911. He reopened the Opera House in 1912 and made improvements, increasing seating capacity to 450. He also increased the size of the stage, added new scenery, repapered the walls and repainted the advertising curtain, moving the projection booth to the back of the theater, out of harm's way.

McElroy offered crude, flickering silent movies, but his Opera House was primarily a playhouse, with live acts arriving frequently via Lubbock's new rail service. At least nine theatrical companies came to town in his first season (1912–13).

When a pestilence of flies threatened theater attendance one summer, McElroy offered a deal to customers. Each Friday morning, a free movie

Bill Payne operated the Opera House between 1909 and 1911. *Courtesy Southwest Collection, Special Collections Library, Texas Tech University.*

ticket would be issued "to every child between the ages of one year and thirty-five who brings with them 100 or more dead flies." McElroy stressed that "no one would be admitted carrying live flies."

Air-conditioning would not come to Lubbock for many years, so the Opera House was quite uncomfortable during hot weather. To accommodate his loyal customers, McElroy established an open-air movie theater, the Airdome, on a vacant downtown lot for two summer seasons (1912–13). The Airdome was the predecessor to Lubbock's drive-in movie theaters, but many customers arrived in horse-drawn buggies.

McElroy decided that Lubbock needed a proper movie house, and his idea produced the first big bright lights in a small dark town. In 1913, he established the Lyric Theatre on Texas Avenue at a prime location across the street from the Lubbock County Courthouse, and the Opera House soon disappeared.

The Lyric was known primarily as a movie theater, but McElroy offered its stage for civic events and live performances, such as song-and-dance act the Christian Sisters and a temperance lecture by Quincy Lee Morrow. On one occasion, McElroy hired Bomar Moore, the town's champion wrestler, to battle a muzzled bear on his stage. The theater opened its doors one Sunday morning for the Downtown Bible Class, which continued to meet there for many years.

The Lyric enjoyed great success, so, in 1917, McElroy moved the theater to a new building a couple of doors to the north, at 1112 Texas Avenue, and signed the first ten-year lease in the history of Lubbock real estate. Meanwhile, he traveled to Chicago and commissioned a $700 state-of-the art sign that boldly flashed "Lyric." Once erected, people came from miles around just to gaze upon the "big modern moving electric sign." The bright lights of the theater attracted South Plains residents to the silver screen for almost fifty years.

In 1918, the *Avalanche* praised the advancement in local film entertainment. "McElroy now runs three reels of new pictures every night, while heretofore he only ran two. This…will no doubt be greatly appreciated by those who attend the moving picture show in this city."

McElroy remembered the first movie he saw in Lubbock, a 1911 five-reel Italian production, *The Fall of Troy*. Popular stars of those early days were Flora Finch, a character actress; dramatic actresses Constance and Norma Talmadge; actor Francis X. Bushman; and the ubiquitous comedian Charlie Chaplin.

*Above*: First location of the Lyric Theatre, west side of Lubbock square, circa 1918. *Courtesy Ken Sharpe.*

*Right*: The Lyric Theater, circa 1934. *Public domain.*

Admission was cheap, as little as ten cents, but McElroy's cost to screen a movie might be six bucks, so a full house of four hundred customers could bring a tidy thirty-four-dollar profit.

Chartered trains would run at intervals from Crosbyton for big attractions and road shows at the Lyric. McElroy recalled the play *The Modern Eve*, for which he charged a dollar for admission. Forty seats had been reserved for passengers on the special train, but by time of the big day, 120 tickets had been sold in Lorenzo alone, so the enterprising theater owner set up chairs in the aisles and put benches in front of the stage to accommodate everyone.

Oscar Phillips ran a confectionery in the front of the Lyric. He rigged up an added attraction by way of a mezzanine at the back of his sweet shop, where patrons could sit at tables and watch movies, with soft drinks and popcorn sent up by way of a hand-operated dumbwaiter.

McElroy sold the Lyric in 1925, and the business passed through several ownerships. He entered the building and loan industry, raised five children and died in 1974 in Lubbock at age ninety-four.

Monumental change came to the Lyric with a glowing advertisement in the *Lubbock Daily Journal* of June 13, 1930, announcing that an "aeroplane" would fly over Lubbock dropping circulars and dozens of passes to a new show. The show was the Lyric's proud entry into talking pictures. On Sunday, June 15, *Flight* began a four-day run. Released by Columbia nine months earlier, the drama starred Jack Holt, Ralph Graves and Lila Lee.

The Lyric burned in 1934. An article in the *Lubbock Avalanche* reported an "opinion" that someone in the balcony—where African American customers were segregated—likely dropped a cigarette and started the blaze. A motor in the building had caused a small fire earlier in the week.

After repairs, the theater reopened in 1935. In the 1940s, the Lyric featured many singing-cowboy movies, then it seemed to fall into decline. In 1956, *The Dancing Legs of a Honky Tonk Hostess* was advertised as "an adult picture of easy-money girls." One of the Lyric's last ads was for *Tarzan Goes to India*, in 1963. Admission was twenty cents for kids and forty cents for adults.

The Lyric closed in 1964. In 1965, the property was purchased by former Lubbock County judge Bill A. Davis. His wife, Paula—Lubbock's first female building contractor—razed the theater and erected a two-story office building, where Davis maintained his law practice until his death in 2000. Their daughter, retired judge Paula Lanehart, recalls remnants of the theater during demolition, including charred traces of the fire and a problematic sloping recessed floor that had to be filled.

Judge Lanehart fondly remembers the years she spent practicing law with her father on the footprint of the old theater, noting, "We probably enjoyed as much comedy there as the Lyric customers!" The property is now occupied by attorney Ted Hogan.

## THE EVOLUTION OF LUBBOCK COUNTRY CLUB: FROM CLOVIS MAN TO BEN HOGAN

One of Lubbock's first important cultural institutions is still in existence, Lubbock Country Club (LCC), established in 1921. LCC evolved when local sportsmen who formed the short-lived Lubbock Golf and Gun Club earlier that year decided a more proper organization was in order.

Thirty-five men met at the Lubbock County Courthouse and arranged to purchase 160 acres on Blackwater Draw, about three miles north of the town square. It was a perfect spot for Lubbock's first golf course and country club.

LCC's 160 acres have witnessed thousands of years of significant history. The earliest of New World inhabitants lived here. Clovis man flourished in Blackwater Draw some thirteen thousand years ago, followed by generations of other cultures, including Folsom, Portales and Archaic period occupants. Clovis points have been found among the bones of ancient mammoth, camel and sabretooth cats hunted by early peoples who visited the area. At LCC, bones from extinct *Bison antiquus* were discovered in the 1980s. People from the Archaic period some three thousand years ago "cropped" the huge beasts into Blackwater Draw, where the animals were killed and slaughtered.

In the 1500s, a contingent of Coronado's expedition searching for the elusive lost cities of gold is believed to have camped near LCC in Blackwater Draw. In the 1870s, buffalo hunters skirmished with a band of Comanche warriors near LCC. By 1880, sheep ranchers occupied these 160 acres. In 1898, George Wolffarth purchased the property.

Wolffarth was a founding father of Lubbock County, its first county clerk and something of a Renaissance man. He married Lottie Hunt, daughter of Estacado Quaker pioneers, and the young couple built a frame farmhouse at Blackwater Draw, where four of their nine children were born. George planted potatoes, an orchard of plums and peaches, alfalfa for his cattle, corn, rye and other grains.

*Left*: George C. and Lottie Wolffarth deeded the land to Lubbock Country Club on November 1, 1921. *Author's collection.*

*Below*: The original LCC clubhouse was situated near the banks of a large lake designed for fishing and duck hunting. *Author's collection.*

Wolffarth established a tree nursery that eventually provided hundreds of tall, fast-growing locust trees to settlers seeking shade. His trees covered the courthouse square. Long before electricity or refrigeration, water from a windmill was piped into a room of the Wolffarth home, where it flowed through a trough in which jars of milk were cooled. The large pond on the property yielded fish for many meals, and a few shotgun blasts could bring down dozens of tasty ducks for a big family dinner. Early land agents used Wolffarth's homestead as a prime example of what fine agricultural and social opportunities could be had for customers interested in settling the South Plains.

Wolffarth was one of the thirty-five men who founded LCC, along with many of the original movers and shakers of the town. The founders envisioned a man's retreat for hunting, fishing, camping and golf. The earliest published LCC bylaws contained more rules governing fishing than any other club activity, including golf.

By 1923, Lubbockites were kicking up their heels in the new clubhouse, which featured a dance hall and a commercial kitchen. Hunting and fishing activities faded, and LCC became the favored spot for local social functions. The *Lubbock Avalanche* chronicled luncheons and dinners, teas and receptions, dances and bridge parties. The newspaper touted the club as a great place to entertain for business purposes.

By the 1930s, golf dominated LCC's activities. When superstar golfer Walter Hagen visited the club in 1931, it was the rough equivalent of Phil Mickelson showing up today at the local miniature golf center. In 1935, LCC hosted the inaugural Women's West Texas Golf Tournament.

Future World Golf Hall of Famers Byron Nelson and Ben Hogan played an exhibition at LCC in 1937 and spent the night in the golf pro's home on club grounds. The twenty-sixth annual Texas Professional Golf Association Tournament was held at LCC in 1946, and one competitor was Harvey Penick, later a famed golf coach and writer. In 1951, LCC hosted the Women's Texas Amateur, witnessed by a thousand spectators.

Meanwhile, LCC built a magnificent swimming pool in 1929. Still in use, the pool is the oldest in Lubbock. Tennis courts were installed by 1934. In the 1960s, LCC tennis pro Quinn Connelley helped popularize the sport locally. Connelley's efforts culminated in the construction of a state-of-the-art indoor tennis facility known as "The Barn," one of the first of its kind in the state.

Unfortunately, LCC was part of institutional discrimination that permeated the South for generations. Minorities were routinely excluded until the 1970s, and widows of members were the only women permitted membership.

Today, LCC—still member-owned—has many women and minorities among its 999 members, and the facility hosts many inclusive social and sporting events. The 1923 clubhouse gave way to a ten-thousand-square-foot, two-story building in 1948 that has been remodeled and enlarged several times over the years. The current fifteen-thousand-square-foot structure and pristine championship golf course make LCC one of the finest country club facilities in West Texas.

## SOUTH PLAINS MOVIEMAKING

Marilyn Monroe never visited the Llano Estacado, but her character Cherie certainly did. In the 1956 movie *Bus Stop*, Cherie describes a journey with her baby sister. "I just picked her up and took her along here, this line," she says, tracing her route on a road map. "Until we got to Lubbock, Texas!" She tells of working in Lubbock at (the fictional) Liggett's Drug Store, winning second place in a talent contest and heading for Hollywood.

*Bus Stop* is just one of many films connected to West Texas and the South Plains. Some movies tell stories about the area but were filmed elsewhere. Others were filmed in the area but depict other locales. A few were shot "on location" and set in the region.

The year 1956 was a banner time for Texas-themed films. Although Lubbock is but a tiny footnote in the plot of *Bus Stop*, West Texas is featured prominently in two classic movies from that year, both listed in the National Film Registry: *The Searchers* and *Giant*.

*The Searchers* was inspired by the true Texas tale of the 1836 abduction of Cynthia Ann Parker by Comanches and her eventual rescue. The movie is set on the Llano Estacado but was filmed primarily in Monument Valley, Arizona/Utah. Directed by John Ford, the film stars John Wayne and Natalie Wood.

In *Giant*, West Texas is transformed from cattle country to big oil. Featuring Rock Hudson, Elizabeth Taylor and James Dean, the epic was filmed in and around Marfa and is one of the few films set and shot in West Texas. A line memorable to locals has the hero's daughter "wanting to go to Texas Tech."

In 1958, *The Big Country* featured an all-star cast, including Gregory Peck, Carole Baker and Charlton Heston. Set vaguely in the mid-nineteenth-century West, cattlemen feud over land and water, with romance as the underlying story. Much of the action takes place in "Blanco Canyon." There is but one Blanco Canyon—in Floyd and Crosby Counties—yet nothing in the

Lubbock is but a footnote in *Bus Stop*, starring Marilyn Monroe, 1956. *Public domain.*

movie resembles the real canyon. The film, shot in Arizona and California, sometimes accurately depicts South Plains vistas of vast plains and waving grass. But often, incompatible mountains are seen on the horizon.

The 1963 Western *Hud*, starring Paul Newman, was filmed at Claude and the historic Goodnight Ranch in the Panhandle. The movie was nominated for seven Academy Awards.

Starring Dustin Hoffman and John Voight, *Midnight Cowboy* is a 1969 drama about two down-and-out buddies in Manhattan. Opening scenes were shot in Big Spring, and the movie won an Oscar for Best Picture. Acclaimed 1971 drama *The Last Picture Show* was shot on location at Archer City. Geographically, Archer City lies east of West Texas, but the film certainly depicts the feel of a 1950s West Texas oil town. Based on the Larry McMurtry book, the film received eight Academy Award nominations.

Another movie set and shot in West Texas is 1975's *Mackintosh and T.J.* It was singing cowboy superstar Roy Rogers' last picture, filmed at the historic 6666 Ranch in rural King County. Rogers said of the movie, "There's no leading lady, no shooting, some fights, but no blood spurting, and that's the way I wanted it." The film spawned a memorable Waylon Jennings soundtrack album that includes his megahit "Bob Wills Is Still the King" and the Bob Wills's song "(Stay All Night) Stay a Little Longer," performed by Willie Nelson.

The 1978 picture *The Buddy Holly Story* starred Gary Busey. Set in Lubbock, the biopic was filmed in California and Georgia. The popular movie drew praise for realism, as actors sang and played their own instruments. Busey was an Oscar nominee for Best Actor, and the film won Oscars for Best Adaptation Score and Best Sound. But South Plains residents were amused by depictions of mountains on Lubbock's skyline, and Holly fans were disturbed by many other inaccuracies. The inaccuracies were addressed in a 1987 documentary, *The Real Buddy Holly Story*, produced by Sir Paul McCartney, featuring Sonny Curtis and Jerry Allison, with many scenes shot in Lubbock.

Bud Davis—John Travolta's character in the 1980 film *Urban Cowboy*— is from Spur, but scenes of his hometown were shot four hundred miles south in Wallis, Texas. The 2000 Tom Hanks blockbuster *Cast Away* begins and ends at a remote road crossing, shot near Canadian in the Texas Panhandle.

Several movies feature brief references to the South Plains. The 2006 film *Glory Road*, set in El Paso, chronicles the 1966 Texas School of Mines journey to basketball greatness. On the way to winning the NCAA championship with five black players, the team wins games in Lubbock's Municipal Coliseum.

The Oscar-nominated 2016 neo-Western *Hell or High Water* is set primarily on the South Plains, with Lubbock the headquarters of the Texas Rangers. Other West Texas towns are portrayed, including Jayton, Tulia and Childress. Depictions of Post and of rural Garza County—where climactic scenes are set—seem familiar, but the movie was filmed in eastern New Mexico.

*Leap of Faith*, a 1992 comedy-drama starring Steve Martin and Debra Winger, tells the story of a corrupt faith healer stranded in the fictional drought-stricken town of Rustwater, Kansas. It was shot in Plainview, Groom, Claude, Happy and Tulia, and South Plains residents were recruited as extras for the movie. Minor roles in the film were played by little-known actors who would rise to stardom: Liam Neeson, Philip Seymour Hoffman and Lukas Haas. Rock star Meat Loaf played a bus driver.

Several Plainview scenes were filmed at what was then called the Quick Lunch Cafe, now known as the Broadway Brew. According to location manager Bill Bowling, the café was chosen for its "feeling of interest. It has architectural integrity of the period. It is not plastic. It is one of a kind."

One scene was filmed at Plainview's Granada Theater. Morning film dailies were reviewed at the Jimmy Dean Museum auditorium. The monarch butterfly scene was shot in Tulia, and a tent revival scene was shot in Groom.

In 2017, at the twenty-fifth anniversary celebration of the filming of *Leap of Faith* in Plainview, director Richard Pearce said the area was chosen "not only because of its photogenic big sky West Texas landscape but also because it seemed to sit at the literal epicenter of one of the country's driest agricultural regions. Plainview would be the perfect place to set this fictional story of a small town experiencing a devastating drought.

"The only problem was that by the time we arrived to actually shoot the movie, the town of Plainview had had one of the wettest springs that anyone in the town could remember. The result was that no matter where you looked, the fields around Plainview were bright florescent green with the 'miracle' of dryland agriculture."

Lubbock lawyer Helen Liggett was chosen as Winger's photo double. Helen's eight-year-old daughter, Anna Liggett, appeared as the blond girl being held up in the final scene of the movie.

Helen said, "Steve Martin was very gracious, but ironically I never met Debra Winger." She gushed, "I got to meet Meat Loaf! Way cool for me as I am a huge 'Rocky Horror Picture Show' fan."

Helen took vacation time and spent about eight days filming over two weeks in Plainview. She remembers being paid, but not how much, and she was disappointed she did not get a screen credit. "The only scene I really recall

Lubbock architect Michael Martin was chosen as photo double for Steve Martin in *Leap of Faith*. *Courtesy Michael Martin*.

was the one filmed from atop a silo of the truck being driven by Mike Martin—Steve Martin's double—with me as the passenger: not very exciting."

Lubbock architect Michael Martin heard children and adults were wanted as extras and took his two kids to Plainview for tryouts. With bushy prematurely gray hair and a similar build, Michael could easily pass for Steve Martin at a distance. He found himself in a waiting room of Steve Martin and Debra Winger look-alikes, called in one by one for auditions.

Michael was chosen as Steve Martin's photo double and describes the experience as "a prolonged whirlwind," working ten to twelve hours a day, six days a week, with all meals provided, during an eight-week period in the summer. "I worked with several stand-ins for Debra Winger, but I recall one special day working with Helen Liggett," said Michael. "We were waiting for a camera to be carried up to the top of a grain elevator. Several kids approached us for our autographs. I'm not sure that they believed we were the 'real' Steve and Debra. I whispered to Helen, 'Let's just give them the autographs. I'll sign my own name. You sign Debra Winger and it will raise her esteem in the community.'

"The first day I met Steve Martin, I was placed in front of the Hale County Sheriff's Office. The director instructed me to exit the building, get in the truck and drive off. I rehearsed it several times. They radioed Steve to the set. We introduced ourselves and the director gave him instructions. They called 'Action!' Steve tried what I had been doing, but the director didn't like his driving. Steve hopped in the passenger side and said, 'Okay, Mike, show me how you did it!'"

Michael remembered shooting an opening scene of the movie on his last day of work. "It was just about dawn as I loaded up with the latest Debra stand-in for a parade through Happy. I'm not sure what the population of Happy was at the time, but all of them and more lined the highway and waved ecstatically, as the cameras rolled. We repeated the same thing several times.

"I know where I appear in the movie, but that is a show business secret. If I told you, I would have to kill you," Michael joked. "The movie didn't achieve perfection, but everyone in the area, including myself, enjoyed its making."

## WOODY GUTHRIE'S PAMPA

Most remember Woody Guthrie as an Okie, but he was inspired by his years in the Texas Panhandle town of Pampa. He lived there only eight years, but Pampa's influence on the young man and his music is undeniable. In the same way Lubbock was slow to embrace Buddy Holly as a hometown hero, Pampa neglected Woody's connection to the town for decades.

Woody wrote the patriotic anthem "This Land Is Your Land" and countless other important works: folk songs, poems, essays and books. He was also known for his impressionistic paintings and drawings. His legacy inspired generations of musicians, artists and writers.

The famed folksinger was born Woodrow Wilson Guthrie in Okemah, Oklahoma, in 1912. His middle-class family suffered tragedy when Woody was fourteen. His mother was institutionalized and in 1929 succumbed to Huntington's disease, a hereditary neurological disorder. Woody's father moved to Pampa for work, and he soon sent for his son.

The teenage Woody attended Pampa High School but seemed uninterested in academics. He spent many days reading at the public library and hung out at Harris Drugs downtown. There, he worked as a soda jerk and discovered a guitar in the back room. His uncle taught him to play the instrument, and a local musician taught him to play harmonica. Woody soon formed his first band, the Corn Cob Trio, and performed with the Pampa Junior Chamber of Commerce Band.

Woody quit school his senior year, took up sign painting and in the evenings played music in local clubs and radio stations. In 1933, he met and married sixteen-year-old Pampa girl Mary Jennings, the sister of a bandmate. They lived in a modest shack and had three children.

But trouble was on the horizon when the Great Depression and the Dust Bowl dealt a double blow to the Panhandle. When the great dust storm of April 14, 1935, hit town, the locals thought it marked the end of the world. The haboob inspired Woody's memorable song "So Long, It's Been Good to Know You."

Woody Guthrie (*far left*) and the Pampa Junior Chamber of Commerce Band in 1936 in Pampa, Texas. *Courtesy Getty images.*

In his autobiography, Woody recalled, "Pampa was a Texas oil boom town and wilder than a woodchuck." The Texas Panhandle country influenced his music and his words. "A world close to the sun, closer to the wind," he wrote. "The cloudbursts, floods, gumbo muds, the dry and dusty things that lose their footing in this world, and blow, and roll, jump wire fences, like the tumbleweed, and take their last earthly leap in the north wind."

As the Great Depression deepened and drought persisted, Woody joined thousands of other "dust bowl refugees." He hitchhiked and rode the rails to California, where he hoped to earn a living. His family remained in Pampa.

In Los Angeles, Woody found work playing hillbilly music at radio station KFVD, gaining a measure of fame. There, he met influential leftists and began writing a column for the communist newspaper *People's World*. The radio station tired of Woody's political views, and he was fired, ending his short California career. He returned to Pampa, and while Mary and the kids were happy to have him back, the restless young hobo soon headed east to New York City.

In New York, Woody's career took off with music gigs, radio performances as the "Oklahoma Cowboy," recording deals and published writings. Mary and the children left Pampa and joined Woody in New York, but the couple divorced in 1943.

Woody loved Pampa, but even after he made it big, the affection was unrequited. When he visited Pampa, he was treated "like an outcast, rumors swirling that he was handing out Communist pamphlets and talking against God," according to a biographer. Woody defended his politics: "I ain't a Communist necessarily, but I have been in the red all my life."

Woody inherited his mother's fatal illness, Huntington's disease, and he was institutionalized from 1956 until his death in 1967 at age fifty-five.

In 1992, a Pampa Chamber of Commerce member suggested the town should take advantage of its connection to Woody. Few thought it was a promising idea, and someone hissed, "Woody Guthrie was an atheist and a Communist!" Nevertheless, the idea caught on, and Pampa hosted the first annual Tribute to Woody Guthrie on October 3, 1992, which Governor Ann Richards proclaimed as "Woody Guthrie Day" in Texas.

Woody Guthrie.
*Public domain.*

A coalition of Pampans purchased the old Harris Drugs building in 2001 and created the Woody Guthrie Folk Music Center. The back room accommodates a stage for jam sessions and music festivals. Walls are covered with Woody memorabilia: newspaper clippings, maps of Pampa highlighting Woody-era landmarks, music festival posters, photographs of Guthrie relatives who have visited (including son Arlo, a famed musician) and a representation of Guthrie's guitar, with its famous motto: "This Machine Kills Fascists."

As late as 2013, the *Texas Observer* reported that Pampa schoolchildren were taught patriotic songs, but not "This Land Is Your Land." When a resident was asked when Pampa would be more accepting of Woody's legacy, she replied, "Maybe 50 years from now."

## The King of the Cowboys: Roy Rogers' Hungry Life on the Llano Estacado

Leonard Slye left Lubbock in 1933 at the low point of his career. "I was so poor I could not even pay attention," he said. But his prospects improved—dramatically.

Leonard Franklin Slye was born in Cincinnati, Ohio, in 1911. As a child, he lived modestly with his family on a rickety houseboat his father built. Years later—as Roy Rogers—he personified the cinematic cowboy, with his guitar, white hat, fringed shirt and fancy boots, riding his beautiful palomino, singing Western songs, righting all wrongs. For decades, the "King of the Cowboys" was everyone's hero.

Leonard's parents often hosted neighborhood square dances. Young Leonard played the mandolin and sang, learning to yodel and call square dances. When the Great Depression hit, the Slye family found its way to California, where Leonard drove a truck and picked peaches.

Overcoming terrible stage fright, he auditioned for an Inglewood radio show in 1931. Leonard sang and played guitar, mandolin and banjo. He was hooked on show business.

The next day, he joined a local country music group, the Rocky Mountaineers, which included the talented Bob Nolan. After Nolan quit the group in 1933, Leonard formed the O-Bar-O Cowboys with Tim Spencer, "Slumber" Nichols and two others. In an old Pontiac, they embarked on a disastrous tour of the Southwest.

The O-Bar-O Cowboys, 1933. *From left to right:* Cyclone, Leonard Slye, Uncle Joe, Tim Slumber Spencer and Bill Nichols. *Public domain.*

During Depression-era hard times, few could afford live entertainment. Drawing tiny audiences, the band struggled to pay for gasoline as it barnstormed through Arizona and New Mexico in the heat of summer without air-conditioning. Leonard recalled, "We starved to death on that trip. We ate jackrabbits. We ate anything we could get to eat."

Reaching Roswell, the group performed on local radio to promote its act. The Cowboys complained about how homesick they were and mentioned favorite foods, hoping someone might take pity. Leonard said he missed his mother's lemon pies. A caller to the station promised that if Leonard would sing "The Swiss Yodel," the caller would bake him a pie. The O-Bar-O Cowboys enthusiastically performed the song.

That evening, young Arline Wilkins appeared at the motor court where the boys were staying, bearing freshly baked lemon pies. Romance blossomed, and in 1936, Leonard and Arline married in Roswell, followed by a musical tour of Texas. In 1946, Arline died tragically during childbirth. Leonard later married entertainer Dale Evans, a native of Uvalde.

For a couple of months in 1933, Lubbock was headquarters for the O-Bar-O Cowboys, performing on the fledgling KFYO Radio. The Cowboys played Lubbock's Palace Theater and entertained civic groups, including the American Legion and Lions Club.

Velma Blanton was a high school student in Lubbock at the time and remembered:

> *This was when KFYO was just getting started....*[The Cowboys] *were not making too much money. They would go out to Brownfield and Littlefield and...all these places around Lubbock to play in little theaters and to play dances....I happened to go up with my girlfriend, and that's how it all started.*
>
> *They would thank Mrs. Jones and Mrs. Brown and Mrs. Smith for all the wonderful cakes and pies and fried chicken that they had brought to the radio station, and sure enough, by the power of suggestion, by the end of the next day, there would be all kinds of goodies for them to eat. I prevailed upon my mom to bake her specialty, silk pecan pie, and I took it up to the radio station. And that's how I met Tim Spencer, my husband-to-be.*

John Julian of Lubbock witnessed the band's hard times. Julian was thirteen years old and played mandolin with a friend who played guitar. The boys were invited to play on KFYO with the Cowboys and later visited the band at the hotel they called home. Julian heard the band members joke about hunting jackrabbits for food on their way from California.

The O-Bar-O Cowboys disbanded in Lubbock in 1933. Their stay may have been forgotten had not Leonard Slye, Tim Spencer and Bob Nolan formed the iconic Sons of the Pioneers a year later. Their success eventually vaulted Leonard to extraordinary fame as Roy Rogers: singing cowboy and movie and TV star.

Roy Rogers returned to Lubbock in 1970 to headline the Texas Tech Intercollegiate Rodeo with his wife and costar, Dale Evans. In 1975, Roy's last movie, *Macintosh and T.J.*, was filmed on location at the 6666 Ranch in King County, ninety miles east of Lubbock (not far from the namesake of the Cowboys, the O-Bar-O Ranch in Kent County). Waylon Jennings and Willie Nelson provided the movie soundtrack.

Ironically, in 1969, the former Leonard Slye—who was once so hungry he dined on jackrabbits—launched a national chain of Roy Rogers Restaurants, one of which later opened in Lubbock. Roy Rogers died in 1998 in California.

# ELVIS IMPACTS THE ICONS OF WEST TEXAS MUSIC

Elvis Presley was paid seventy-five dollars for his first performance in Lubbock, but the value of his influence on West Texas music icons proved priceless.

Texans welcomed the little-known swivel-hipped "bop" singer from Memphis with great enthusiasm early in his career. He barnstormed across the state, opening Lubbock's Fair Park Coliseum on January 6, 1955, followed by points beyond: twenty-six-plus appearances in West Texas that year.

"I owe a lot to Texas," Elvis told a reporter. "They're the ones who put me over the top." He said: "I've covered a lot [of territory], mostly in West Texas. That's where my records are hottest. Down in San Angelo, and Lubbock, and Midland, Amarillo."

Elvis returned for many Lubbock bookings: in February, April, June and October 1955, and in April 1956. In addition to Fair Park, he likely played Lubbock's famous Cotton Club on each of these dates.

Eighteen-year-old Buddy Holly attended Elvis' January 6 stop in Lubbock at Fair Park. On Elvis' February 13 return, Buddy—playing Elvis' acoustic guitar—opened the show with Bob Montgomery, who played Buddy's soon-to-be iconic Fender Stratocaster. Buddy reportedly drove Elvis around town sightseeing that evening. Buddy and bandmates opened for Elvis twice more that year at Fair Park. These gigs led to a contract with Decca Records, eventually resulting in Buddy's rise to fame with the Crickets and as a solo performer. "Without Elvis none of us would have made it," said Buddy.

Elvis and Buddy never met again, but after Buddy's tragic death in 1959, Elvis sent a telegram of condolence from Germany. He called Buddy his "favorite rock 'n' roll singer."

Seventeen-year-old Sonny Curtis of Meadow witnessed Elvis' appeal at his early Lubbock performances. "None of us had ever seen anything like Elvis, the way he could get the girls jumping up and down, and that definitely impressed

Elvis Presley takes a break during his second Lubbock appearance, February 13, 1955. *Public domain.*

Buddy Holly," the Rock & Roll Hall of Famer remembered. "But it was the music that really turned Buddy around. He loved Presley's rhythm—it wasn't country and it wasn't blues—it was somewhere in the middle and it suited just fine. After seeing Elvis, Buddy had only one way to go, rock 'n' roll."

On February 13, 1955, at Fair Park Coliseum, seventeen-year-old Waylon Jennings of Littlefield met Elvis backstage. "Elvis was just jumping around everywhere, bouncing and bubbling over with enthusiasm, full of more energy than anybody I ever saw. He was talking to me like he'd known me a thousand years," Waylon recalled. "I was crazy about Elvis. I loved that churning rhythm. He didn't even have drums yet, but the rock 'n' roll part was unmistakable."

Waylon, a founder of Outlaw Country, recorded dozens of country hits. He is a member of the Rockabilly Hall of Fame and the West Texas Walk of Fame.

Roy Orbison was on the front row of Elvis' February 16, 1955 show at Odessa High School. The eighteen-year-old from Wink was looking for showmanship pointers he could use for his own group, the Wink Westerners. "His energy was incredible; his instinct was just amazing. There was just no reference point in the culture to compare it," Roy recalled. He became an instant Elvis fan and appeared with Elvis on KOSA-TV in Odessa.

Roy, a Rock & Roll Hall of Famer, recorded numerous hits, including two number-one hits and ten top-ten hits. Elvis referred to Roy as the "greatest singer in the world." Roy was the only performer who opened for both Elvis and the Beatles.

On June 3, 1955, Elvis gave a free show at Lubbock's Johnson-Connelley Pontiac dealership preceding his performance at Fair Park. Among the hundreds who witnessed the performance was thirteen-year-old Mac Davis of Lubbock. "That's when I knew what I wanted to do with my life: play music," Mac recalled. Every performer who ever performed in rock and roll is lying if they tell you that they weren't influenced by Elvis Presley. He turned the world around."

Years later, Mac wrote multiple hit songs for Elvis, including "In the Ghetto," "Memories" and "Don't Cry Daddy." He is a member of the Songwriter's Hall of Fame and West Texas Walk of Fame. "Elvis been berry, berry good to me!" joked Mac.

When Elvis performed in Amarillo on October 13, 1955, twenty-two-year-old Buddy Knox of Happy attended the concert and afterward met the headliner backstage. Elvis encouraged Knox to record, declaring prophetically that rock 'n' roll was "fixing to happen." Knox took Elvis' advice and released a string of hits in the 1950s and '60s, including the number-one hit "Party Doll." The two stars later bumped into each other during their service in the U.S. Army, and Elvis welcomed Knox and his wife to his Graceland home. Knox is a member of the Rockabilly Hall of Fame.

Elvis performed to seven sellout crowds in West Texas between 1972 and his untimely death in 1977. He was forty-two.

## LUBBOCK'S BOBBY LAYNE: THE ULTIMATE GOOD OL' BOY

Lubbock has been home to many big-name entertainers, athletes and other celebrities, but few chose Lubbock as a place to retire. When football great Bobby Layne retired to the Hub City, his activities here became the subject of perhaps as many legendary tales as those he inspired on the gridiron.

Born in 1926, Bobby was a native of tiny Santa Anna, Texas, near Coleman. He was a star high school football player at Highland Park in Dallas.

He was one of the most successful quarterbacks ever to play for the University of Texas. Bobby was selected to four straight All-Southwest Conference teams from 1944 to 1947 and was a consensus All-American in his senior year. At UT, Bobby met Carol Krueger, daughter of prominent Lubbock physician J.T. Krueger and his wife, Leila. By 1946, they were married and living in Lubbock.

Bobby was the third overall selection in the 1948 NFL draft, and by 1950, he was starting quarterback for the Detroit Lions. In 1952, he led the Lions to their first NFL championship in seventeen years.

Bobby was notorious for off-the-field antics that flew in the face of general NFL conduct and behavior, but his skills on the field made him one of the best quarterbacks of his era. He perfected the two-minute offense. He said: "I never lost a game. Time just ran out on me."

The Lions won two additional league championships with Bobby before the Super Bowl era. He scouted and coached awhile, then retired to Lubbock in the early 1960s. On his retirement, he held every NFL passing record. He was inducted into the Pro Football Hall of Fame in 1967.

He was perhaps the ultimate West Texas good ol' boy: a superb athlete, a world-class party animal, a shrewd businessman and a family man in his spare time. In Lubbock, Bobby was involved in farming, bowling alleys, real estate, oil and the stock market. "I like Lubbock a lot," Bobby said. "There's not much to do there except go to somebody's house or the country club, but I like the people. They don't give a damn if I play football, I'm just Bobby Layne.

Bobby Layne. *Author's collection.*

"I probably would have played ball another year or two if it hadn't been for this place and my family being here....Lubbock's my home and it got a little harder to leave every season."

Baseball icon Mickey Mantle was one buddy Bobby regularly invited to his base of social operations, Lubbock Country Club (LCC). Another close friend was his attorney, Lubbock lawyer Cleddie Edwards. Cleddie remembered the time Bobby instructed him to entertain Mickey so that Bobby could concentrate on a high-stakes poker game. Cleddie spent a few hours playing an innocent game of dominos with Mickey, because it was the only game Mickey knew. "Mickey wasn't much of a gambler," Cleddie said.

Bobby was a big-time gambler, and poker was his best game. He often played seven days a week. He reportedly won between $200,000 and $750,000 annually playing poker locally. Lubbock grocery magnate Roy Furr was one of Bobby's favorite poker buddies.

Despite Bobby's reputation for late nights of partying, he was an early riser, especially to play golf, hunt or fish. "I sleep fast," Bobby said. If a hungover buddy complained about Bobby waking him bright and early for an outing, Bobby would always respond, "You gotta learn to play hurt!"

A single-digit handicap, Bobby was a fierce and fearless links competitor, typical of one of the last in pro football to play without a face mask. He loved golf and would always play in LCC's invitational tournaments. His invited guests often included Mantle and football greats Yale Lary, Doak Walker and Rooster Andrews.

One year, the tournament committee hired a group of musicians who entertained from a flatbed trailer near the eighteenth green as the players finished their rounds. As the band played "When the Saints Go Marching In," Bobby led his somewhat tipsy group, including the usually reserved Doak Walker, in a wiggling, twisting boogie across the fairway, with Bobby twirling his golf club like a drum major, abandoning all golf balls to the course.

In 1981, Bobby was seriously considered as head football coach at Texas Tech, but the job went to Jerry Moore.

It is perhaps appropriate that Bobby's most famous words reflected his hard-charging lifestyle. "The secret to a happy life is to run out of cash and air at the same time." A quote often attributed to his buddy Mickey Mantle is said to have originated with Bobby: "If I'd known I'd live this long, I would have taken better care of myself."

Bobby Layne lived in Lubbock until his death in 1986 at age fifty-nine. Some said he did not die. Time just ran out on him.

# 7

# CATASTROPHE, CELEBRATION AND A STATESMAN

## THE SOUTH PLAINS STRUGGLED THROUGH THE SPANISH FLU PANDEMIC

Between 1918 and 1920, the Spanish flu killed as many as fifty million people worldwide, one of the deadliest pandemics in history. A half million Americans died, including about twenty-five thousand Texans. Residents of the Texas South Plains were struck hard by the virus.

No reliable statistics have survived, so it is not known how many Lubbock residents fell ill from influenza, but at least ten died. (Ten deaths amounted to 0.25 percent of the city's 1918 population. By comparison, by February of 2021, COVID-19 had killed 0.23 percent of the city's population.) A review of local newspaper accounts illustrates an eighteen-month epic struggle with a silent killer in rural Texas.

Lubbock was a small town in 1918, with a population of less than four thousand, and fewer than ninety thousand people occupied the twenty-four counties of the Texas South Plains. Most lived in farming communities.

Radio broadcasts would not reach the South Plains for several years, so newspapers were the only form of mass communication available to disseminate health warnings, official proclamations and other essential information. The *Lubbock Avalanche* was published weekly, so updates were delayed.

World War I soldiers were the first Americans struck by the illness, and news of the impending crisis appeared in the *Avalanche* on September 26, 1918. "Spanish influenza has made its appearance in at least 25 army camps

Lubbock Sanitarium's first nursing class poses in front of the sanitarium, 1918. The hospital treated many Spanish flu patients. *Courtesy Southwest Collection, Special Collections Library, Texas Tech University.*

over the country. The surgeon general's office announced tonight that the total number of cases has increased to 20,211, including 2,225 new cases reported today. Seven camps reported influenza for the first time today."

On October 10, several flu illnesses were reported in a dispatch from the Center community, and the first death in Lubbock was published in the *Avalanche*. "Mrs. D.R. Cypert died Friday afternoon of pneumonia, developing from a severe case of influenza. Deceased's husband was unable to accompany her remains, as he was also sick of the same trouble."

A week later, the epidemic forced local authorities to shutter the city for two weeks, as reported by the *Avalanche*. Mayor C.E. Parks ordered all public places and gatherings closed.

> *All public and private schools, music classes and other places of instruction, churches, societies, clubs, club-meeting, picture shows, lodges, club rooms, and pool and billiard halls shall be closed, and business and social entertainments, public gatherings and people gathering and congregating on the streets, in business houses, hotels and restaurants, except for the transaction of such business as shall be absolutely necessary, be and the same are hereby prohibited.*

Grocers, hotels and restaurants remained open with specific instructions for sanitary services, including "articles shall be sterilized or boiled after using and before serving another person therewith."

When the shutdown ended, a front-page *Avalanche* article, "Epidemic Is Still Raging, But Physicians Believe Conditions Are Improved," outlined rules for healthy behavior: "Have sufficient fire in the home to disperse the dampness. Open your windows at night. If cool weather prevails, add extra bed clothing. Boil all dishes."

An attempt to combat the crisis with wartime humor appeared in an October 31 letter to the *Avalanche*:

> *I am just recovering from a severe attack of that fearful disease that the Kaiser has introduced in this country called the Spanish "Influence." How he can command so much "badness" is more than I can understand. First it was the "German Measles." The next trouble I am looking for him to send over here is the "Turkish Catarrh" and the "Bulgarian Gout." But what we most need right now is a "Universal Peace" and a cessation of arms. Everybody in these parts are about over the "Influence" and are busy saving their crops.*

Lubbock schools reopened in mid-November with a hopeful comment in the *Avalanche*: "It is the general opinion that all epidemic is well spent, and the greatest danger is now passed."

The optimism soon faded, and the December 12 *Avalanche* was filled with bad health news and multiple flu obituaries on the front page. The mayor reinstated a strict city shutdown through December 29, with violators facing fines of up to twenty-five dollars.

When restrictions ended, the *Avalanche* reported "quite a number of flu cases developed," but public gatherings and church services resumed. Meanwhile, the newspaper itself was "badly handicapped," as employees were struck by influenza.

As the epidemic continued, an editorial in the January 16, 1919 *Avalanche* expressed frustration that the "very best authority was bested" by influenza. The newspaper questioned whether the Lubbock City Commission's restrictions were of any use. "It seems that it has had little effect on stamping the disease out of the community."

Over the next year, however, the *Avalanche* published only a smattering of news articles concerning the influenza epidemic, and there were no official announcements restricting schools, churches or public gatherings.

Advertisements for dubious patent-medicine flu remedies were common, including Scott's Emulsion, Peruna and Dr. Pierce's Pleasant Pellets.

By 1920, the Spanish flu epidemic was over, making way for the Roaring Twenties.

## LUBBOCK'S CELEBRATION OF VICTORY IN WORLD WAR II

August 14, 1945, was a day downtown Lubbock seemed to quake, as a cacophony of honking can-dragging cars, whistles and horns, fire sirens, church bells and shrieks of a population described by the *Lubbock Avalanche-Journal* as "hog wild, pig crazy" celebrated the end of World War II.

Like the rest of the world, residents of Lubbock and the South Plains suffered devastating losses from the deadliest conflict in history. Among the twenty-two thousand Texas servicemen killed or missing during 1942–45, about eight hundred were South Plains residents. This number does not include thousands of South Plains combatants who were wounded or captured. The *A-J* devoted an entire page of many editions to "News from the Men Serving in the Armed Forces of Uncle Sam."

On the homefront, South Plains residents were quick to support the war effort, but it required many sacrifices. Federal rationing meant meat, sugar, coffee, shoes, rubber and auto parts were in short supply, and gasoline was available only on certain days. Prices and wages were controlled by the government, which also banned production of certain consumer goods, including appliances, automobiles and new housing.

Residents were peppered with seemingly endless pushes to purchase Series E bonds to help fund the government's multitrillion-dollar war effort. In June 1945, the *A-J* reported that Lubbock County had reached only a third of its war bond sales goal of $1,700,000.

On the other hand, the war meant renewed prosperity for a region devastated by the Great Depression. In 1941, the Lubbock Army Air Corps Advanced Flying School opened west of town, creating many jobs for local civilians. Later renamed Lubbock Army Airfield, the base brought thousands of GIs to Lubbock to train on military aircraft. Lubbock Army Airfield graduates went on to fly in every theater of the war. Many thousands of additional GIs were trained as glider pilots at South Plains Army Airfield north of Lubbock between 1942 and 1945.

WACs (Women's Army Corps) march in downtown Lubbock to promote the sale of war bonds during World War II. *Courtesy Don Abbe.*

The South Plains then, as now, was a center of agricultural activity. With prices high, farmers cultivated the soil to its maximum, helping the United States feed and clothe the Allies. Cotton farmers earned an average of $997 per crop in 1939 and $2,894 in 1945, a 190 percent increase. The area oil industry saw a similar boom.

But the stress of World War II far outweighed any benefit war brought to the local economy. Everyone was eager for the end of the great conflict. The beginning of the end of the war was V-E Day, commemorating the Allied victory in Europe, on May 8, 1945.

The *A-J* reported a mostly somber reflection on the grand accomplishment, with no parades or similar celebrations on Lubbock's V-E Day. The city virtually closed shop, but downtown streets were deserted. Everyone seemed to flock to churches on that Tuesday to offer prayers of thanksgiving, including 1,000 people at First Baptist, 750 at First Methodist and 250 at First Christian.

Conspicuously absent were the uniformed figures of soldiers. With the victory proclamation at 8:00 a.m. came an order that all military personnel stationed at Lubbock Army Airfield were restricted to the field for twenty-four hours.

With the war against Japan still raging, residents realized V-E Day was but a partial victory and seemingly held their collective breath for final victory. There was still work to do. Three months later, on August 14, the announcement finally came that Japan had surrendered. Lubbock immediately exploded in wild extemporaneous celebration of V-J Day (Victory over Japan Day). Blocks of downtown Lubbock were snarled with vehicles and crowds. Fireworks crackled and pistol shots were fired into the air, accenting the beat of the surging population.

Among the revelers were veteran soldiers from Lubbock Army Airfield sporting overseas decorations and vying for attention from girls in the crowd. According to the *A-J*, "Two young girls were seen running down the street and straight into the arms of a couple of lieutenants. One of the girls tripped and found herself around the feet instead of the neck of her intended. But it was all in fun and who cared? The crowd laughed and went merrily on its way."

Alcohol was illegal in the "dry" town of Lubbock, but many liquor bottles were seen in the open rather than "under the table," as was noted under ordinary conditions.

There were also sober religious services the evening of V-J Day, as thousands took time to attend church to offer expressions of thanks for the end of war.

August 14, 1945, marked a fresh start for millions of Americans who had suffered through sixteen years of the Great Depression and almost four years of war. In Lubbock, the war effort sparked the city's economy and growth, as the population more than doubled during the decade (1940 census was 31,853, 1950 census was 71,747), making Lubbock the second-fastest-growing city in the United States.

## George Mahon:
## Greatest of West Texas Statesmen

He tops the list of the *Lubbock Avalanche-Journal*'s "most influential people of Lubbock's 20th century." The Hub City's federal building, a park and the downtown public library bear his name, and his legacy marks historic growth of South Plains infrastructure, agriculture and commerce. So, who was George Mahon?

Born in 1900, George Herman Mahon was one of eight children in a poor Louisiana farming family. The family soon moved to rural Mitchell County, Texas. He graduated from Loraine High School, Simmons College (now Hardin-Simmons University) and the University of Texas School of Law. He was licensed as an attorney in 1925.

Mahon was elected Mitchell County attorney in 1926 and was appointed district attorney of the 32nd Judicial District in 1927. In 1932, the new 19th Congressional District was created, which included Lubbock County. Mahon, a Democrat, announced his candidacy for the seat and in 1934 defeated Judge Clark Mullican of Lubbock in a runoff.

Mahon spent the next forty-four years in the House of Representatives. His was among the longest and most distinguished of congressional careers.

He served on congressional military committees and was considered one of the best-informed people in Washington on matters of national defense. After Japan's Pearl Harbor attack in 1941, Mahon predicted, "The Lord willing, the day is coming when we are going to smash Japan off the map." Was his statement hyperbole or prophesy? He was one of the half dozen men in Congress trusted with knowledge of the Manhattan project, begun in 1939, for the development of the atomic bomb. However, Mahon probably first learned specifics of the bomb project in 1943.

As a delegate to Democratic National Conventions from 1936 to 1964, Mahon participated in the selection of party presidential nominees from FDR to LBJ. His seniority and political influence led to his 1964 election as chair of the House Appropriations Committee, making him one of the most powerful men in U.S. politics, though he was never well known to the general American public.

A fiscal conservative, Mahon worked throughout his career to limit government spending, but he showered his home district with prize political projects. His efforts led to the establishment of Reese Air Force Base in Lubbock and Webb Air Force Base in Big Spring. In 1969, he established funding to create Interstate Highway 27. The highway, 124

President John F. Kennedy
with George Mahon, circa
1961. *Courtesy Southwest
Collection, Special Collections
Library, Texas Tech University.*

miles long, was a huge boon to transportation and commerce for Lubbock,
Amarillo and beyond.

Mahon never forgot he was a West Texas farm boy and played an
important role in the development and continued funding of agricultural
and energy programs throughout his years in Congress.

Reflecting his constituency, he was a social conservative, though
he supported some of Roosevelt's New Deal ideas. He opposed the
desegregation of public schools ordered in 1956 by the Supreme Court
in *Brown v. Board of Education*. He supported the House Un-American
Activities Committee's anticommunist investigations of the 1950s and
LBJ's Vietnam War. He opposed 1960s civil-rights legislation, Johnson's
Great Society programs and gun control.

In 1923, Mahon married Helen Stephenson, and the couple had one
daughter. They bought a home in Colorado City in 1926 and maintained it
for the rest of their lives, though they also claimed Lubbock as a hometown.

The Mahons were known for their hospitality, warmly welcoming
constituents and other visitors in Washington. He taught Sunday school
at Metropolitan Memorial Methodist Church in D.C. and maintained
membership in First Methodist Church of Colorado City.

In 1978, Mahon decided not to run for reelection. His House seat was claimed by Lubbock Democrat Kent Hance, who defeated Midland Republican George W. Bush in the general election—Bush's only election defeat. Hance said of Mahon, "Of all the people I've met in my lifetime, he best fits the definition of a gentleman. Mahon was loyal to his friends and accommodating to his foes. He always tried to use a persuasive manner to get people on his side."

He might casually address President Truman as "Harry" and on the same day humbly address West Texas farmers and reporters as though they were heads of state. Mahon seemingly never forgot a name or a face. He did not drink, smoke or use strong language. Even LBJ—well known for his use of profanity—watched his tongue in the presence of Mahon.

Mahon biographer Janet Neugebauer said, "I never heard him brag... except one thing. He said, 'I have the most nonpartisan committee in Congress.'"

In 1985, at age eighty-five, he died following complications from knee surgery. A large Washington delegation attended his funeral services at First United Methodist Church in Lubbock. He was interred at Loraine Cemetery. His widow died in 1987 and was buried beside her husband.

George Mahon was certainly a product of his time and his constituency. Despite perceived political flaws, he should be remembered as the greatest of West Texas statesmen.

# SELECTED BIBLIOGRAPHY

Abbe, Donald, and Paul H. Carlson. *Historic Lubbock County an Illustrated History*. San Antonio, TX: Historical Publishing Network, 2008.

Abbe, Donald, Paul H. Carlson and David J. Murrah. *Lubbock and the South Plains: An Illustrated History*. Chatsworth, CA: Windsor Publications, 1989.

Apel, Dora, and Shawn Michelle Smith. *Lynching Photographs (Defining Moments in American Photography)*. Berkeley: University of California Press. 2008.

Baker, T. Lindsay, and Billy R. Harrison. *Adobe Walls: The History and Archaeology of the 1874 Trading Post*. College Station: Texas A&M University Press, 2001.

Bronwell, Nancy. *Lubbock a Pictorial History*. Self-published, 1980.

Caldwell, Clifford R., and Ron Delord. *Eternity at the End of a Rope: Executions, Lynchings and Vigilante Justice in Texas, 1819–1923*. Santa Fe, NM: Sunstone Press, 2015.

———. *Texas Lawmen, 1835–1899: The Good and the Bad*. Charleston, SC: The History Press, 2011.

Carlson, Paul, and Donald R. Abbe. *The Centennial History of Lubbock Hub City of the Plains*. Donning Press, 2008.

Carr, Joe, and Alan Munde. *Prairie Nights to Neon Lights: The Story of Country Music in West Texas*. Lubbock: Texas Tech University Press, 1997.

Carrigan, William D., and Clive Webb. *Forgotten Dead: Mob Violence against Mexicans in the United States, 1848–1928*. New York: Oxford University Press, 2017.

Crosby, Alfred W. *America's Forgotten Pandemic: The Influenza of 1918*. New York: Cambridge University Press, 2003.

Cutter, Paul F. *Early Lubbock*. Fort Worth, TX: Eakin Press. 1991.

Graves, Laurence. *A History of Lubbock, West Texas Museum Association*. Lubbock: Texas Technological College, 1963.

Griffis, Ken. *Hear My Song: The Story of the Celebrated Sons of the Pioneers*. Northglenn, CO: Norken, 2001.

Guralnick, Peter. *Last Train to Memphis: The Rise of Elvis Presley*. New York: Back Bay Books, 1995.

Guralnick, Peter, and Ernst Jorgensen. *Elvis Day by Day: The Definitive Record of His Life and Music*. New York: Ballantine Books, 1999.

Gwynne, S.C. *Empire of the Summer Moon: Quanah. Parker and the Rise and Fall of the Comanches, the Most Powerful Indian Tribe in American History*. New York: Scribner, 2011.

Hardorff, Richard G. *Cheyenne Memories of the Custer Fight*. Lincoln, NE: Bison Books, 1998.

Holden, William Curry. *Alkali Trails: Social and Economic Movements of the Texas Frontier, 1846–1900*. Lubbock: Texas Tech University Press, 1998.

James, Bill C. *Jim Miller: The Untold Story of a Texas Badman*. Wolfe City, TX: Henington Publishing Company, 1983.

Klein, Joe. *Woody Guthrie: A Life*. New York: Delta, 1999.

Lynn, Alvin R. *Kit Carson and the First Battle of Adobe Walls: A Tale of Two Journeys*. Lubbock: Texas Tech University Press, 2014

McVay, Freda, and Ashton Thornhill. *Lubbock City of Land and Sky*. Memphis, TN: Towery Publishing, 1994.

Michno, Gregory F. and Michno, Susan J., *Circle the Wagons!: Attacks on Wagon Trains in History and Hollywood Films*. McFarland & Company. 2017.

Neal, Bill. *Death on the Lonely Llano Estacado: The Assassination of J. W. Jarrott, a Forgotten Hero*. Denton: University of North Texas Press, 2017.

Neely, Bill. *The Last Comanche Chief: The Life and Times of Quanah Parker*. Wiley, 1996.

Neugebauer, Janet, and Kent Hance. *A Witness to History: George H. Mahon, West Texas Congressman*. Lubbock: Texas Tech University Press, 2017.

Newcomb, William Wilmon. *The Indians of Texas: From Prehistoric to Modern Times*. Austin: University of Texas Press, 1961.

O'Neal, Bill. *Encyclopedia of Western Gunfighters*. University of Oklahoma Press, 1991.

Philbrick, Nathaniel. *The Last Stand: Custer, Sitting Bull, and the Battle of the Little Bighorn*. New York: Penguin Books, 2011.

Phillips, Robert W. *Roy Rogers: A Biography, Radio History, Television Career Chronicle, Discography, Filmography, Comicography, Merchandising and Advertising History, Collectibles Description, Bibliography and Index*. Jefferson, NC: McFarland & Company, 2009.

Rogers, Roy, and Dale Evans. *Happy Trails: Our Life Story*. New York: Simon & Schuster, 1994.

Rogers, Roy, and Georgia Morris. *Roy Rogers: King of the Cowboys*. New York: Collins Publishers, 1994.

Shirley, Glenn. *Shotgun for Hire: The Story of "Deacon" Jim Miller, Killer of Pat Garrett*. Norman: University of Oklahoma Press, 1970.

———. *Temple Houston: Lawyer with a Gun*. Norman: University of Oklahoma Press, 1980.

Spivey, Broadus, and Jesse Sublett. *Broke, Not Broken: Homer Maxey's Texas Bank War*. Lubbock: Texas Tech University Press, 2014.

Stadler, Gustavus. *Woody Guthrie: An Intimate Life*. Boston: Beacon Press, 2020.

Sullivan, Roy F. *Kit Carson at the First Battle of Adobe Walls*. Bloomington, IN: AuthorHouse, 2015.

Tune, Bernice. *Golden Heritage and Silver Tongue of Temple Lea Houston*. Fort Worth, TX: Eakin Press, 1981.

Ward, Ed. *The History of Rock & Roll*. Volume 1, *1920–1963*. New York: Flatiron Books, 2017.

Wert, Jeffry D. *Custer: The Controversial Life of George Armstrong Custer*. New York: Simon & Schuster, 1996.

Wood, Amy Louise. *Lynching and Spectacle: Witnessing Racial Violence in America, 1890–1940*. Chapel Hill: University of North Carolina Press, 2011.

# INDEX

# ABOUT THE AUTHOR

Chuck Lanehart is a criminal defense lawyer based in Lubbock, Texas. In his forty-three-year career, he has represented citizens accused in almost the entirety of the Texas Plains and beyond. Thirty years ago, he began writing about the rich legal and cultural history of the region. His history articles and essays have been featured in many publications, including legal journals and newspapers. In 2008, he was named among the "200 Most Influential People in the History of Lubbock" by the *Lubbock Avalanche-Journal*.